ABUSED *but* NOT BROKEN

Ashle' Bell

Abused but Not Broken
Trilogy Christian Publishers
A Wholly Owned Subsidiary of Trinity Broadcasting Network
2442 Michelle Drive
Tustin, CA 92780
Copyright © 2023 by Ashle' Bell

Scripture quotations marked (AMP) are taken from the Amplified® Bible, Copyright © 2015 by The Lockman Foundation Used by permission.

Scripture quotations marked (KJV) taken from *The Holy Bible, King James Version*. Cambridge Edition: 1769.
For information, address Trilogy Christian Publishing
Rights Department, 2442 Michelle Drive, Tustin, CA 92780.
Trilogy Christian Publishing/ TBN and colophon are trademarks of Trinity Broadcasting Network.
For information about special discounts for bulk purchases, please contact Trilogy Christian Publishing.
Manufactured in the United States of America
Trilogy Disclaimer: The views and content expressed in this book are those of the author and may not necessarily reflect the views and doctrine of Trilogy Christian Publishing or the Trinity Broadcasting Network.
10 9 8 7 6 5 4 3 2 1
Library of Congress Cataloging-in-Publication Data is available.
ISBN: 979-8-89041-123-5
ISBN: 979-8-89041-124-2

DEDICATION

The book is dedicated to a few people:

My two heartbeats, Zion and Tavaris Jr. You have seen me at my lowest and darkest moments, you've cried with me, hugged me, comforted me, and loved me through my pain. You didn't fully understand what I was dealing with or why, but you never judged me or left my side. I apologize for the traumatic experiences and pain I caused. I know you wanted to see your mother happy and not sad for a change. Look at us now, we have made it to a better life, and now you get to see me smile and be all that God has called me to be.

Marvin Bell Sr., Nancy Cole, and Keshia Tooks-Riley, you all left to be on with the Lord, but what you have done for me will forever be etched in my memory. Having you as a part of my life has been a joy and I pray that I have made you proud.

Those who have suffered in silence and passed way due to abuse. Those who are currently suffering in silence with no hope. I want you to know that there is hope in Christ and this book is written just for you.

FOREWORD

By Laquisha Swain-Mitchell

Prepare yourself to witness firsthand a powerful journey told through bravery and courage. Ms. Bell (Ashle') eloquently narrates a series of her real-life events, bringing you into her experiences through transparency and truth. The feeling of inspiration consumes you and somehow it lingers. You get to know her as she testifies. And she leaves you with a heartwarming sense of respect and astonishment.

PREFACE

I am not a licensed therapist or counselor, nor do I claim to know it all, but I am a woman who has experience. Writing this book took a lot of courage, strength, and boldness. I knew this story needed to be told when we see so much death in the world and in many cases it's due to domestic violence or some form of abuse. He placed the assignment on me to get this book done and like Jonah, I ran away from it many times. But over the last year, it became clear that there was an urgency. The fire and passion that grew inside of me had me getting journals and starting this journey into being an author. I share some of my experiences with you and invite you into some of the most intimate moments of my life so that you can understand those who are abused and the things that go through our minds. As you read this, do so with an open mind and ask the Holy Spirit what He would like you to take from this and apply it to life.

ACKNOWLEDGMENTS

OMG.... This was hard because there are so many that have made an impact on my life and brought things out of me that I never knew existed. I know I will leave a lot of you out and I ask that you please, please, please forgive me. Don't charge it to my heart, charge it to my brain because my life has been a journey. I am forever grateful and thank each one of you.

TO MY TEACHERS AND STAFF MEMBERS OF THE SCHOOLS I ATTENDED:

Mrs. Holman and Mrs. Davis (Redemptive Life Academy), Mrs. Dillard, Ms. Brown, and Ms. Hart (Roosevelt Middle School), Mrs. Smith, Mr. Hands, Mrs. Fong, and Ms. McQuade (Palm Beach Lakes High School), along with many others each of you supported me and pulled out the intelligence you knew I had. You believed in me and pushed me to go further in my education. Thank you!

FRIENDS AND IMPORTANT PEOPLE:

Sabrina Walls, girlllllll words could never express my love for you and your family. You saw me, loved me, and supported me every step of the way. God knew exactly what He was doing when He had us cross paths. You and your family are stuck with me for life. Thank you!!!!

Abused but Not Broken

Tiffaney Johnson, LaDawn Grant, and Melody Towns each of you have been there for me in many different ways. Thank you for the rides, the hugs, the listening, the encouragement, and the love you have shown me. You helped me by being there when I was going through the toughest times. Thank you!

Mrs. Desiree Jackson, my work mom and mentor, you knew it all without me speaking, you didn't judge me, you just loved me. You helped me keep my job and encouraged me to get free. You have known me since I was a child, and you paid attention to me when I thought I was invisible. You would pull me into your office and pour into me countless times. Thank you!

Rhonda Hunter, I have known you for years but never knew what a friendship with you would be like. You were one of the first people God allowed me to befriend when I came out of separation. You listened, encouraged, prayed, and never judged me. Thank you!

My Wake Up & Pray family and the McTear family, you all met me after my transition to Christ, but I must acknowledge how supportive you have been when I told you I was writing a book. The prayers, phone calls, text messages, and encouragement has been phenomenal. Thank you!

Kim Mathis, SISSSSSSSS OMG I do not even know where

Acknowledgments

to begin. You believed in my vision, the phone calls, the text messages, the trip you blessed me with so I could get away to write, telling me about Trilogy Publishing and then convincing me to contact them. When I told you they approved of my book the excitement and joy you shared with me was just unexplainable. And the crazy part about it is I have not even met you in person yet, but we danced together and praised God together… Thank you, Sis!! (WOW)

Hellon Singletary, my mentor, my confidant. You met me after all the chaos, I approached you and asked you to be my mentor after observing you at church and serving with you. You saying 'yes' was one of the best things to ever happen. When I sat down with you for the first time and gave you an overview of my life, you said I should write a book and I told you it was coming soon. Thank You!!

Ore'al Bluntson and Shawntaye Gaines, my dear sisters in Christ. It is so much I can say about our relationship. God knew what He was doing when He placed us together. The love, support, correction, vulnerability, and growth are priceless. My prayer warriors, thank you!!

Apostle Trevor and Pastor Martha Banks, you welcomed me into the family at Resurrection Life. Thank you for the prophetic words concerning me being an author, meeting with me, and praying with me when I told you I began writing the book. Thank you!

FAMILY:

Grandma Wilhelmenia, my best friend and weekend partner. Being with you taught me so much, you were my escape and breath of fresh air when I needed to get away from the chaos. Thank you!

The Richardson family, words could never express how grateful I am to you for everything you have done for me and my children. Thank you!

Mom, thank you for always opening your doors for me and my children. Thank you for accepting my change and believing in me. Thank you!

Tavaris Sr., the father of my children, we have been through so much from the time we met, but you have always been there for me and our children. You believed in me and supported me with everything. You knew things weren't always good, but you never pushed the issue, you just told me you got me. You are the best co-parent and friend a woman could ever have. Thank you!

To the rest of my family, I love y'all dearly. You may or may not know my struggles or battles because I hid them well, but I appreciate you for being there if I ever needed you.

Rhett, Michele, and the whole Trilogy Publishing staff, including the editors and designers, what an honor it has

Acknowledgments

been to work with you from start to finish. I did not know what to expect when I first reached out, but I am so glad that I did. Every time fear tried to creep in you gave me confidence that I was heading in the right direction. Thank you all for helping me to deliver my "baby," I am forever grateful.

Last, but definitely not least, Abba Father, Lord Jesus, and the Holy Spirit, thank You for choosing me. You loved me when I didn't love myself. You saw me when I didn't see myself. You chased after me until I realized it was You that I needed all along. I commit my life and vow to worship you all my days. You deserve all the glory, honor, and praise!!! THANK YOU!!!

TABLE OF CONTENTS

Dedication... 5

Foreword.. 7

Preface.. 9

Acknowledgments.................................. 11

Introduction....................................... 19

Chapter 1: The Backstory 23

Chapter 2: John 10:10a The Thief................ 33

    The Planted Seed............................. 34

    He Came To Finish 39

Chapter 3: John 10:10b The Lifegiver 67

Chapter 4: Separation 73

Chapter 5: Do You See What I See? 83

Chapter 6: R&R (Rebuild & Restore) 89

Chapter 7: You Are Not Alone 111

Prayer 117

Afterword 119

About The Author................................. 121

INTRODUCTION

No one wakes up and says, "You know what? I am looking forward to the day that I get abused." So please don't judge or make assumptions about someone when you don't know their story. Abuse is something that develops over time and once you realize you are a victim of abuse, you find it hard to escape because it is a cycle you find yourself lost in. There is a process and steps that need to be taken when trying to get out, it's something like being addicted to a drug. There are highs and lows, ups and downs, just like a rollercoaster ride. No, you don't love the pain or the torture, but you love the person, the thrill, and the potential you see in the person, and you feel as if you can help the person. This person is also someone close to you that you have known for years. There is a stronghold and soul tie that keeps you stuck and feeling helpless.

Abuse can be broken down into many categories and depending on the person and situation it can leave a devastating or even tragic impact on them. Also, depending on your culture and background, this can be looked at as an expression of love or a badge of honor. Yea, I know it may sound crazy but coming from where I'm from this was the norm. It was laughed about and joked about so much that those of us who were being abused became numb to it to a certain extent. We didn't speak up about it because it was better left unsaid, and you didn't want to put people in your business like that.

Most people who meet me are shocked when I share my story with them. I hid my pain very well behind smiles, pictures, achievements, etc. I didn't feel comfortable or safe enough to discuss my pain with many people out of fear of judgment and negative comments. People always say what they will never do or allow anyone to do to them, but truth be told no one really knows until faced with it. I grew up in a somewhat toxic environment and witnessed abuse, so when you get into an abusive situation you think it's normal.

See me, I'm Ashle' (pronounced Ash-lay), and I was a victim of abuse, I say was because abuse no longer defines me, for I am a new creation and all old things have passed away. I have witnessed quite a few forms of abuse such as verbal abuse, emotional abuse, physical abuse, mental abuse, and financial abuse. I want to take you through a journey of my life to show you how I went through abuse and was able to overcome it. The cycles I went through took me years to untangle and get set free totally. My story is unique and one of a kind, death was knocking on my door for years……. but GOD! The journey you are about to take with me will expose you to some very delicate matters that formed the scars that made me who

Introduction

I am today. The scripture found in Romans 8:28 most definitely comes into play when looking at my life and how it all unraveled.

So, before we set sail, let me say this: I am not here to bring shame or blame anyone for the decisions or choices that I made. I take full responsibility for my role and the part I played in these situations. I'm not perfect and I did make many poor choices in life however, what did happen to me I did not deserve, I was looking for love, not pain. So, with that being said LET'S GOOO (you know how they say when people be cheering on their favorite team)!!

CHAPTER 1:
THE BACKSTORY

Most people say life is what you make it. And I can agree to some extent because we are in control of how we react and respond to situations, and we are in control of those we choose to surround ourselves with. However, we cannot control what happens to us. As children, we are brought into a family that we didn't choose, so we become influenced by them and adapt to the culture and environment they laid out for us. Sometimes, this can be good and then there are times when this can be bad; it just depends on who your family is and how you are raised.

I know you may be wondering, *who is Ashle' and why should I listen to anything she has to say?* Well, I am glad you asked, I want to take a few moments to share with you who I am by letting you into my world. This is a long overdue story but fear, worry, and a host of other things kept me back from sharing. I am just like you in some ways, I have had my share of ups and downs. I had my promiscuous phase which lasted for a few years, and I cleaned myself up and got back on track. I had my moments of vengeance and being nasty to people because of how they treated me. The crazy thing is I couldn't keep up with being that way to save my life, lol. At heart, I am a cool down-to-earth, loving, caring, loyal, and authentic, woman. I am unique, a one-of-a-kind and to truly know me is to love me.

I grew up in the average family, single mom with two kids, working to pay bills and take care of us. We were well taken care of financially and did not want for much. Everything we wanted we pretty much got. I have a huge family on both my dad's and my mom's side. There was a lot of love given in tangible ways, but not the love I felt I needed. I often felt invisible by some and over-recognized by others. Communication was not our best attribute. A lot of things would be said and swept under the rug causing voids to be left. I felt like they overcompensated with money and materials things because they lacked other important life skills. I could be wrong but that is my opinion and how I saw it.

Overall, I had a good childhood for the most part because I was surrounded by my cousins and siblings who were close in age. We got into a lot of mischief and chaos but hey those were some of the best days of my life, the laughter, the joy, the craziness of growing up with those

Chapter 1: The Backstory

who are your first friends in life. I loved to be around people and make them happy with laughter. I got pleasure from making others smile. I had some great relationships on both of my parents' sides of the family. Even though I never got to experience a two-parent household, I had both of my parents actively involved in my life. My relationships with each of my parents were different though.

I would go and visit my dad from time to time and I even had a chance to live with him for a while, just thinking about that brings me joy because those were the good old days. In 2010, my father passed away so, I no longer get to make new memories with him, but I get to reflect on the good times. I would consider myself more of a daddy's girl. My dad would do just about anything I asked, and he would make me feel as if I was his only child. Even though there were many of us, he had a special relationship with each one. No child was left behind, my dad was a rolling stone, to say the least, but he had a big heart and would do whatever it took to make you happy.

My relationship with my mom was a little bit of the opposite, we had good moments but there was always a struggle. We could never really see eye to eye on a lot of things. It was like a love-hate relationship that I could never really understand. We would find ourselves in heated arguments that would sometimes turn into physical fights. But I trust she did the best she could do raising two little girls as a single mom and working as a beautician all hours of the night. So, I just went with the flow of things and didn't put too much into it. And now that I am older, new memories are being created.

I was an honor student and loved to read books (I still do to this day). I liked to escape into a different world and have a different life from time to time. Because even though I was surrounded by many, I felt so alone. I felt like I could never just be my true self. I had to live up to other people's expectations and do what others felt I should do. It was tough but I was good at putting up a front and just getting the job done. People thought that life was just great because my deception was just that real.

From elementary to high school, I excelled in my classes and was complimented by many, and even landed a college scholarship. I was determined to be someone in life and make my family proud. I mean with all the pressure I had at times why not give them something to cheer for and take pleasure in? I didn't let any of the personal matters I was dealing with get in the way or stop me from reaching my goals. There were some delays along the way, but I got there.

At the age of thirteen, I found out I was pregnant with a baby. This was a big shock to my entire family, because no one knew I was sexually active, so their finding out

Chapter 1: The Backstory

showed just how secretive I was during this season of my life. The whole story behind the pregnancy was life-changing. Later in life, I felt this was a move of God because He knew what I was experiencing at the time and what I needed in my life.

My great-grandma Nancy had just passed away in November 1999. She and I were very close, it was like she was my best friend. We spent so much time together. I would go to the "package" store for her when needed and so many other things. She was my everything, she protected me and just loved on me like no other. She would let me sleep in her chair and just sit with her watching "The Price is Right," "In the Heat of the Night," Murder She Wrote" and so many other shows. I get emotional just reflecting on her and the memories we had.

She always kept me close to her. Especially at times when I would get hurt or injured myself. I remember the time I set fire to my Jheri curl trying to be like Michael Jackson in that Pepsi commercial, she hurried to put me in the tub so that the fire could die out, she cared for me and made sure I was good. Also, when I was running around the house with my cousins and burned myself on the electric heater, she helped nurse me back to health as my skin would peel off. Grandma Nancy probably got tired of my clumsiness and silliness, but she never said it and I never felt it. She did what she needed to help me and just let me be me.

She became ill with old age and was placed into a nursing home where she would eventually end up passing away. I would go and visit her there at times but never expected my last visit to be my last visit. The news of her passing away devastated me. I went numb and something inside of me died. To be honest, I didn't want to live another day because life was already tough. And it got tougher because now I didn't have my safety net anymore. Even though I had a short time with her, it was pure and genuine love. She did not play about me and made sure people knew it. Her passing had me behaving recklessly, which led to me getting pregnant.

So, here I was thirteen in the eighth grade expecting a child to be born in August 2000 from a dude that was not thrilled about it and didn't want anything to do with me once he found out I was pregnant. That story is a whole testimony, I won't have time to dig into it but just know with God things turned around for the better and he not only fathered one, but both of my children and we became great friends in the end.

But, let me pause right quick and tell y'all how this whole discovery of me being pregnant came about, it wasn't funny then but it's funny now:

I knew I was pregnant before anyone else because I

Chapter 1: The Backstory

just knew my body and it was acting funny, not eating, and being tired all the time. My mom must have been catching on because one night she started to ask me questions, such as why I'm not eating and why I haven't asked for any pads for my menstrual and so forth. I answered with my lies and thought, *okay maybe she would leave me alone,* but I was wrong. She then told me to eat dinner, I didn't want it, but she forced me to eat. I will never forget it was fried chicken, yellow rice, and green beans. The food smelled disgusting to me, and I knew if I ate it, I wouldn't be able to keep it down. So, I just took a few bites hoping that would satisfy her but nope, she had me eat more until I couldn't take it anymore and ran to the bathroom.

So, the next day I am getting ready for school thinking everything is back to normal. Boy was I in for a surprise. I was terrified come to think of it because we passed by my school and pulled up to the Planned Parenthood building a few blocks down. I began to panic because now, I'm like the truth is about to come out and I wasn't prepared nor ready for this. Long story short I go in get tested and guess what?......... I was pregnant!

My mom was livid and made me call my father right away from the clinic phone. Now knowing the kind of relationship, I have with my dad, this was one of the hardest conversations I ever had to have with him in my life. I had to actually say the words to him. So, here's a snippet of that conversation:

> ME: Hello, Dad, my mom wanted me to call you because we are at this clinic.
>
> DAD: Okay Ashle', so what's going on?
>
> MOM (in the background): Go on and tell him with your grown behind, don't be scared now.
>
> ME: The lady gave me a test and I am pregnant.
>
> DAD: WHAT? PREGNANT? Ashle' what do you mean? Who is the boy that got you pregnant? I need to talk to him now!
>
> ME: It's this boy I have been going with and okay... (I begin to cry at this point)
>
> DAD: I am taking you down to the welfare office and putting you on welfare. How are you going to take care of a baby? You need to pack up your stuff because you are coming to live with me, and no more talking to boys.
>
> ME: Okay (in between sobs)
>
> MOM: takes the phone and they start talking. And she tells him the story of the night before and a host of other things, that I eventually tuned out.

The cat was out of the bag at this point so no more

Chapter 1: The Backstory

hiding or covering it up. I began to share with my friends what happened and then I eventually had to face the rest of my family members and have conversations with them. There was talk of abortion, there was talk of me keeping the baby. I was confused and did not know what to do. My dad and the guy ended up talking and that was not a good conversation either, but years later they turned out to be good friends.

Now back to what I was saying, I entered my freshman year of high school as a mother. I did a lot of soul-searching and doing things to try to find myself and make it through high school. I had friends and family there to support me during this time. One of the key people that taught me so much was my Aunt C. I do not know how I could have managed motherhood if it was not for her. My first couple months of motherhood were challenging but because of her, I was able to get through. Just like when I entered high school with a baby, I left high school expecting my second child. So, my going off to college was out of the question. I attended the local community college in my area and worked to be able to help take care of my family. I went to college longer than usual but that's to be expected when you have kids and life hits you with unexpected turns.

I won't sit here and act like I did not enjoy some parts of my life because I did have my moments of fun.

I lived my life to the fullest in the best way that I could under the circumstances I was in. It's just that some things could have been left out and I would probably be giving a different story. But, by reading this condensed version of my background and how it all began I hope you have gotten to know a little about me before we get into the heart of things.

Every experience was for a reason, every letdown, every setback, every tear was just for you. I have come to learn that our testimony is not just for us but for those that need faith, hope, and strength. So, when you ask me who I am or why should you listen to me, I will say it is all in the title. I was abused, but not broken. I am an overcomer. I am virtuous, I am a mother of two amazing, unique children who has come to know her true value and worth. I am a child of God....

CHAPTER 2:
JOHN 10:10A THE THIEF

In the Bible there is a passage of scripture that sums up this chapter of my life:

The thief comes only in order to steal and kill and destroy.
John 10:10a AMP

So, now that you have gotten to know a little bit about me and my upbringing. It's time we unfold and expose this thief. I want to get to the heart of why you have this book in your hand and can't put it down. For as long as I can remember I had been a targeted attack of the enemy. He wanted to silence me so my voice would not be heard. In an eight-year period, the enemy came in like a flood and just had his way with me. I was so caught up into this whirlwind that I didn't know what hit me. There was a seed planted from childhood that he watered and tilled to start the demise of my life. So, let's start there...

THE PLANTED SEED

I remember it like it was yesterday, that tone of voice I would never forget. "I don't even like you," they said. I shrugged it off like *whatever* and laughed but deep down inside I was torn apart and began to cry internally. I just couldn't let them see me break down because they would think I was weak. I cared and it hurt me deeply inside, but I had to act like I wasn't bothered. They called me "green" (meaning gullible and naïve) for the majority of my life anyways and this would be the icing on the cake for them. I don't remember exactly what happened that led to these harsh words, but what I do know is that they said them and meant it. I guess I was the only one who heard it because no one said anything, or maybe they just ignored it.

This is when it all began to make sense to me, the unkind words, the fighting, the lack of affection and love. The last thing you expect is a close relative speaking to you as if you were an enemy or a non-factor. I began to put up a guard around this person and limit the interactions I had with them as best I could. I felt alone and left out because I don't think I ever did anything to cause them to feel this way about me. I was respectful and kind towards them, but it seemed forced for me to get the same reaction.

As a child, I struggled with being my true self because

everyone expected me to be who they thought I should be. They didn't always tell me exactly, but it was the words that were used when speaking about me or to me. You know how someone can push off their ideas and perception on you in a subtle way. I started forming a dislike for myself because I wasn't living my truth. There would often be some form of comparison between myself and my cousins because I was an honor student, and they weren't. I was called smart, and they would be called dumb or some other words that would be hurtful to them, this added pressure on me because they were my friends, and I didn't want them to feel a way towards me.

All of this led to my first experience of abuse which was emotional. Here I am a young child feeling pressure, mistreatment, controlled, and a host of other feelings because of family. I loved my family and wanted to do whatever I could to make them proud but at times it was just too much for a young girl to handle. A negative light began to shine, and I didn't know what to do, I was trapped in confusion. I was losing my sense of emotions and began to be careless about my own life.

Because of the influence this one person had on me I felt that if they didn't like me then no one else would. It cut me deep inside and caused me to develop low self-esteem, which then targeted my mental. No matter the accomplishments and changes that I made, it was never good enough for them, they always had something to say that left me regretting what I shared or allowed them to know about anything I did. It was confusing, to say the least, because in front of people, they would act differently, but behind closed doors, I got different treatment from them. Imagine being trapped in that closet.

My elementary and middle school years were some of the best because I was able to have a way of escape by interacting with other people outside of my immediate family. I wanted to fit in so I would have to work hard because some saw me as a quiet, smart, shy girl. I wanted to be known for me though, which led me to do rebellious things. Even if that meant losing my virginity at the young age of eleven/twelve. Some would even say I was naïve, but I was really just out there trying to devise a plan to get attention and love from others. I would observe the cool and popular kids to see what they did differently so I can do the same.

We never had the sex talk or anything like that in my family so, I experimented myself and talked about it with friends. My family didn't have the slightest idea that I would be out here having sex at such a very young age. I didn't understand the concept of love, but I felt like I was in love with the young boy I was dating at the time, he told me he loved me, so we set a date and it happened. Of course, he broke my heart shortly afterward, but I healed

Chapter 2: John 10:10a The Thief

from it eventually and moved on. I felt if I did what others wanted me to do, I would get some form of happiness that would satisfy me for the moment.

I would take every opportunity I could to spend less time around the person that was used to start my abuse cycle. I wanted to tell someone how I really felt inside but I was afraid that they would either not believe me or say I was over-exaggerating, so I suffered in silence. I would do my schoolwork and read books as my way of escape. This made me feel better because at least I wasn't being put down and left feeling confused and abused. I became so caught up in how I was viewed by others that I would constantly change my eating habits, dress code, appearance, etc.

I did have a couple of people that didn't add to my pressure and actually loved me genuinely. They just weren't a part of my everyday life, so when I did get to be with them all the cares in the world seemed to disappear. For instance, my cousin KT was more like a mother to me than a cousin. She had an open door for me, and we had a bond that was just amazing. She may not have fully understood or known what I was dealing with, but her love was unconditional. She did so much for me from the time I was born until the day she left this earth. It makes me emotional just writing this because if it had not been for her, I don't know how I would have made it through some things in life. She was one of my confidants along with my Grandma Nancy, and father.

When I was pregnant, KT took me in when I needed a place to go, she helped me get through high school and gave me so much wisdom. She was the one holding my hand as I gave birth to my first child and became the godmother of my second child. I mean whatever I was dealing with she was always there with a listening ear. She motivated me and encouraged me to do more and be more. Even when I may have not liked what she said, she still said it with love, and I had to respect it and take heed of it.

But even with the few good people in my life this one person had the most influence and was the one who controlled my feelings and reactions. I know now it wasn't right but at a young age whose thinking that this would be the door opener to all the other abuse that they would later experience. I always had a heart for people and when I saw them being treated unfairly, I would become empathic and try to do something to cheer them up, because that is what I wanted to be done for me.

So, because of my history and background, I developed an attraction to those who I felt I could relate to due to our similarities. I felt connected to the underdogs and those who felt hopeless or unseen because I too was that person, so I would befriend those people, and the majority of them

Chapter 2: John 10:10a The Thief

were males, I did have some female friends, but I can't say all of them were genuine. Only a handful of them were true friends I could count on, the rest were just associates or people I could hang out with to have fun because the trust, authenticity, and love weren't really there. It's as they say some friends are for a season, lesson, or lifetime. And here I am thirty plus years later and don't even talk to half of those people. And it's no offense to them, it's just showing that the saying is true.

Okay, so I enter adulthood nearly broken, emotionally and mentally abused but with the hope that something is going to change because now I have control of my life or so I thought…....

HE CAME TO FINISH

Here I was in my early twenties with two children, a decent job, a car of my own, and an apartment. I finally was able to move out on my own and now was ready to see what the world had to offer me. I wasn't under the pressure of family as much at this point. I mean they did chime in here and there but because I was on my own, I didn't have to live up to their expectations as much. My children and I were comfortable and happy, bills paid each month, and money left over to do a few extra things we wanted to do as a family.

The little abuse and trauma that I went through before had nothing on what I am about to disclose next. My life had become upside down and been set ablaze and I was so blinded to it that I risked losing it all just to say I was in a relationship and won the fight. What fight you ask? Child, I don't even know because I was the one getting beat. I felt like I had dated the devil himself in different people. It was the same spirits but in different bodies. In the book of Matthew, the Bible talks about how once a spirit is forced out of a body it will leave and go find more spirits that are much stronger and come back into the body and leave the person worse off.

As I speak on these situations, I will refer to these different guys as "him," because remember it was the same spirits but different bodies. It's what you would call familiar and monitoring spirits, they study your life and learn all they can about you so that they can present themselves to you in a different way but still produce the same outcome. You may be thinking *it ain't that deep* but take a moment to examine your life and count how many times you have been in the same situation but with a different person, or how come the same thing happens around the same time each year. You wonder if you will ever get out of this cycle but it's hard because you like what you like. You go after the same type of guys/girls and say you have a type, no baby, you have a familiar spirit that has deceived you and tricked you into thinking

Chapter 2: John 10:10a The Thief

a set way, but anyways, back to the story.

He wanted me dead, and he was willing to use anybody he could to get the job done. He started as my friend and being someone, I could confide in. He understood my pain and felt where I was coming from when I explained my life experiences. He told me that he loved me and would never hurt me. He was the one that I would be able to depend on no matter what. He also needed me because he was dealing with things that only I would be able to understand. These were the people I was attracted to as I mentioned before, there was a connection and I felt I was the one who could help turn things around.

The friendship grew deeper and turned into love (lust, is probably the best term now that I think of it), and from there a relationship formed. We became inseparable and eventually moved in together. He accepted my kids, and I accepted his kids if he had any. We were becoming a family. Life was good, we both worked and took care of the household. I began to feel safe and secure; this was good for me. It wasn't perfect but it was what I had been longing for. We cooked meals together and did family activities, I mean what more can you ask for, right?

As a youth, I wasn't taught anything about financial literacy. All I knew how to do was count it and spend it. We used money as a tool to pay bills and buy cars, clothes, jewels, and whatever else made us happy. I was used to getting whatever I wanted plus more, so there was no real discipline. No one ever said we need to save money for the future. Come to think of it, I don't think I opened my first bank account until I was in my early twenties. I never knew much about saving unless I was saving for my favorite toy or prize possession. So, I would spend it on whatever and whoever. And when in a bind, go to grandma for a bailout.

The enemy was slick here because coming from the society I lived in money is where the power was. You needed to flex and show others how you were living. So, to prove that I wasn't broke I would get money and just blow it on crazy stuff. I can't even recall all the senseless things I purchased. But I remember this one time I spent over $8,000 just in clubs, buying drinks, paying for people to get in, tipping strippers, buying drugs, and whatever else that came with it. I was living this fantasy life that left me broke in the end.

Because I was still suffering inside from previous issues in my past, this brought me gratification and comfort for the time being. I needed to feel needed by people so if someone close to me was in need, I would help them out. I would offer to pay for things and help people financially just to cope with the emotional and mental abuse I was battling. Meanwhile, I am helping to dig a hole that I didn't know I was about to fall into. He

Chapter 2: John 10:10a The Thief

knew I was emotionally damaged already. So, why not target the next best thing that would keep her hostage? Finances.

I struggled with being alone and felt a relationship was what I needed. I was tired of the side-piece relationships and friendships that I had. I wanted desperately to have my own family. So, I would see who I would be able to develop a relationship with and go from there. I didn't know what would be waiting for me on the other side though. Things would start out nice, they would treat me well and present themselves to be the perfect gentlemen. I fell in love quickly because they met the qualifications, I had which I see now were very minimum: have a job, be a family-oriented person, cute (to me), and have some potential (OMG... PLEASE DO NOT FALL FOR POTENTIAL EVER!!).

It did not hit me until I saw a notice from a local pawnshop saying that the payment was past due for something. I remember calling to get more information and then looking in my jewelry box for my necklace, it was a gold nameplate with the word, "Boo" written in cursive. I couldn't find it, so I went down to the pawnshop and there it was my necklace. I was livid and could not understand who would do this and how. I was drawing blanks because I couldn't imagine someone in my house doing this. I had a lot of jewelry from over the years and I was able to choose what I wanted to wear each day. Even though I did not wear it daily, it was mine and not to be touched by anyone without my permission.

At this point, I'm asking questions to find out what is going on, but I am getting lies, such as he doesn't know how it happened, who did it, or what. He blamed friends and even had the nerve to blame the kids. I was shocked that he would even try to say something like that. My kids would never steal from me, let alone they were too young to even pawn something. It was later revealed that it was him who pawned my jewelry. I did get it back and we argued about it and broke up for a little bit and eventually got back together, I'm thinking things would get better because he apologized and said he wanted to do better, however, they got worse.

Money started coming up missing along with more items being pawned such as video game systems, more jewelry, and whatever else he could get his hands on that had some value. Come to find out he had lost his job and had a drug habit he could no longer support himself. So do the next best thing and that is steal from your girl. As you will see later, the newfound drug habit caused so many issues for us because not only did he expect me to support his habit but if I didn't things would get really ugly. I didn't know much about dating a drug addict to begin with. I mean I knew of people who used drugs, but

Chapter 2: John 10:10a The Thief

I never had my own personal experience of dealing with one as a partner. So, it was new to me having to hide my money or possessions from a person so that they could get drugs.

He continued taking my money and car to go buy drugs and hang out with his friends. The car would be on "E," and I was the one responsible for putting the gas back in it. I had to get to work and take my children to school, so I had no choice but to put a couple of dollars in the tank. Whatever money he made would be used to buy drugs but never to put gas in the car. I barely was in my car because he always had it. It was like he became selfish and only was concerned about himself and what he needed. I felt like I was raising three kids and not two and began to get extremely frustrated but didn't have the courage or strength to leave because he had a hold on me.

My finances were going downhill quickly, where before I had enough to make ends meet, now I barely had enough to put food on the table. My bank account stayed in the negative and I was robbing Peter to pay Paul. Every time I got paid it was to replenish what I was negative for and then with the excess I would try to pay for the things needed. This led to me having to do payday loans and ask certain family members for money. It was embarrassing because I had a decent job and was making good money, but I never had anything to show for it.

When I did have access to large sums of money, it wouldn't last long because I would try to get back on track and make up for lost times. I would do things for my children, pay people back the money I owed them, and then try to sneak in something for me before he came and took it away. To escape my reality, I would go out to eat, buy little gadgets that I liked and purchase some books, it never hit me to put money into a spare account until way later down the line. I had terrible spending habits and because of pride, I didn't feel comfortable telling anyone the truth about what was going on. I had to lie to get financial support.

I had to do what I did best, smile and put on a show as if life was great but in reality, I was struggling. I mean I had a "man" in my life, and he was supposed to be helping me. So why should I be asking for help when that was supposed to be his role? I was trying to cover up for him, so he didn't look bad as a man which made no sense at all. He had me thinking poverty was the way to live and I was playing perfectly into his plan. I was in this trance of being this ride-or-die female not paying attention to the death that was waiting around the corner.

I eventually would get behind on my car note and even my rent causing me to face repossessions and evictions. I would have to miss out on certain events because I did not have the funds to participate. I was beginning to

Chapter 2: John 10:10a The Thief

get so stressed out and knew this was not the life I was supposed to be living. Before he came into the picture, I was comfortable and stable, but with him, I turned out broke and miserable.

The mission he set out to accomplish in round one was complete: Steal. He stole all I had and left me to pick up the pieces. I was taken advantage of by someone I trusted and let inside of my world. Instead of me taking a break and recovering, I needed a way of escape, so I did what I felt was the right thing to do go out clubbing, and guess who I ran into, the one who came to kill me mentally.

Remember how I told you I struggled with my self-esteem? I created this fantasy world of mine and hid my pain and emotions behind a smile and extracurricular activities. I would often drink a lot and club as mentioned before. I would be out so late to where all I had time to do was shower and go to work. Dancing and drinking were my thing, even though I wasn't a good dancer, I knew how to work with what I had. I got a lot of attention too, so I was in my element for the time being. Every weekend and some weekdays you would be able to catch me in somebody's club whether it was Mirage in Lake Worth, FL, TKO in West Palm Beach, FL, or Club Boca, in Boca Raton, FL, just to name a few. These were the spots to be in Palm Beach County and everybody would be in the building.

He knew I liked to be the life of the party and my being with him added fuel to that fire. I was in this trance where all I saw was flashing lights and I was becoming popular. He gave me access to a lot of club promoters that would let me get in for free and people that would boost my ego. Popular females and dudes knew who I was and acknowledged me. I felt I was coming out of the darkness into the light, ha, ha, ha (all my Believers know this was the complete opposite). It was my time to shine, and I wasn't going to let anything stop this from taking place. But little did I know a shift was coming that I was not prepared for.

I invested so much into this man and to get treated the way that I did was horrible. I was what you would call a true rider. There was nothing that I would not do to help him and ensure that he was good. He was never wrong in my eyes. So, I stood by this man's side through thick and thin, to the point where I took charges for him. Thank God it wasn't any felony charges, just little minor things that ended up going away. I would have fallouts and disagreements with my family and friends, all because of him.

So, here I am going all out for this man but what do I get in return...him coming home with a used condom on his penis, yes, you read that correctly. He hops into the bed after being out all night so when I go to touch him and

Chapter 2: John 10:10a The Thief

I felt the condom, you can just imagine what was going through my head. I went slap off and punched him dead in the face because for one, you were out cheating and then for two, you get in my bed with another women's residue on you.

The cheating was not with just one but multiple women and unprotected at that. Having babies, exposing me to diseases and infections that could harm me and possibly ruin my life. He would have these women in my car and even the apartments that we shared. He lived a double life and I found myself in this position where I was sharing him with other women voluntarily. We knew who each other were, we had fights but at the end of the day nothing changed, we just shared a man we assumed we loved.

When it came to these women it was tough because they would call me to tell me what he was doing and ask me to help them deal with him and how can they get rid of him. They acted like we were friends at one point with all the conversations we had. And I was close to letting that happen, being that I had a heart for people and didn't want to see anyone hurting. They would express their hurt and pain, meanwhile, I am over here dealing with pain of my own. And trying to figure out how in the world I got in this place and couldn't move from it.

I had the role and title of the main lady, which made no sense, but that's what came with my culture. I was above the baby mamas and side pieces. I held power when it came to important matters, I was on the paperwork and the main point of contact in case of anything. I know it sounds crazy, but you can't make this stuff up. I was going through pure misery but was in too deep and connected that I had no exact route of escape. Anything could happen to any of the other chicks but when something happened to me, or he felt he was about to lose me he would act a fool.

Women would try to see what it was about me that made him choose me over them, but little did they know I was suffering inside; I didn't even know why I was chosen at the time, but here I was playing my position well and hiding behind a title. I didn't feel worthy or even good enough to be chosen because I didn't know my value. I mean, I knew I was a good woman but, I didn't know how good of a woman I was.

To drown out the foolishness of his cheating and being with different women, I started to use drugs, such as ecstasy, weed, and molly. I was so into this relationship that I began to do some things that I'm ashamed to even relive or repeat. I didn't understand the hold that was on me, but I realized it was around the time I became a loner. I would go out to clubs alone and just vibe, I was in a depressed state of mind and didn't want to tell too many people about what was going on. So, the fewer people

Chapter 2: John 10:10a The Thief

around me the better. I would get high with him and just drink the night away, not having too many cares in the world.

I would be out at all times of the night not caring that I had to be at work in the morning. My main focus was to do whatever I could to save my relationship because I didn't want to be a failure and end up alone. My close circle of friends at the time was dealing with the same thing, so they couldn't help me. The people I needed the most were deceased, so I held a lot inside because I was very embarrassed and didn't know who I could really trust. I began just hoping and praying that things would get better because I was dealing with so much and couldn't take any more hurt. Things didn't get better though, they only got worse. He would make me feel so small and tell me how I needed to change certain things about myself and how I was the reason for the cheating.

I turned into this stalker-type female where I'm pulling up to the different spots he is usually at. I would go out to clubs alone just so I could spy on him, I would even GPS his location and go to people's houses or hotels and sit outside waiting for him to come out. I was losing my mind and barely getting sleep. My kids would either be at home or with family. I would come up with excuses for babysitters so I could find out where this dude was and who he was with. I was something like a private investigator, watching every move.

Dealing with all the different women, had me questioning myself and contemplating if I really was the problem. The memories of my childhood began to resurface, and I would see myself as ugly. People would often say I was beautiful and didn't deserve what I allowed, but I didn't see what they saw. Because not too long before I had suffered two ectopic pregnancies in my life and was told it was very rare that I would ever have children again. That hurt me to my core and had me feeling useless as a woman. I mean what man would want to be with me knowing I couldn't have his children; I did try a couple of times and searched for resources but there was no success. I was becoming numb and felt defeated, he was getting the best of me and playing with my mind. Depression crept in strong this time, but I had to find a way out of this rut. I just had to because I was a fighter deep down inside.

So, a little time passes, and I am gaining some strength and boldness. However, I wasn't able to fully recoup because guess who decided to show their face, the destroyer. Packaged just right and delivered to my front door. You would think, *okay she's been through enough so let me give her a break. She was solid and held it down. She endured enough pain, so I will go easy on her this time.* But like I mentioned before he had a job to do. And

Chapter 2: John 10:10a The Thief

like they say in those combat video games, "Finish Her," that is surely what he set out to accomplish.

It all started with a push to the ground. My mind was telling me to go but my heart said stay because he didn't mean it, he just lost his temper. I must have said something I shouldn't have said and pushed the wrong button. I could be very blunt at times and speak without thinking. I just knew that had to be the reason. He apologized and said he would never do it again. We talked it out and I believed him. I just knew that he was going to be good to me this time. We had an understanding and he helped me come out of some tough situations.

However, I was blind to the red flag that was in front of me and did not see anything coming until it hit me dead in the face, literally. The push was the intro to the physical abuse I was about to experience. The charm, apologies, and sweet gestures were all a setup to help me look past what was really unfolding. He was good with his hands (both good and bad) and helped me get a lot of things done I was not able to do on my own. I mean he pulled out all the cards, and his smile was to die for. Looking into his eyes and being able to call him mine took control of my heart and caused me to fall deeper. I began to feel like he could do no wrong and that incident was just an honest mistake.

The physical abuse started out small with the push,

then moved to the twisting and bending of the fingers and hand. It then escalated to choking and strangulation, a way to silence my voice from being heard, which lead to damaged vocal cords. I believe that is why I can't scream or hold a tune anymore (so give me some grace if I sound bad, lol). He knew I had something to say. And then to full-blown punches to any area that was available to access at the time. I experienced so many fights and had to cover so many scars all over some of the dumbest, most insecure things. In the midst of all this, he would take my possessions and leave me stranded with nothing, causing me to ask or beg for them back. It was manipulation in full form but remember I was blind to this.

He wanted full control of my life and if I rebelled or things didn't go as expected, there were consequences. People knew me to be loyal and faithful, but he always felt I was up to no good. Which was dumb because my loyalty is what brought us together in the first place. So, he would check my phone and go through my messages to see who I had been talking to and what I was talking about. I had no privacy at all. If I didn't give access to my phone that is when he would then bend my fingers and twist them until I was in excruciating pain and had no choice but to give the access away.

Once he got inside the phone, he would see that there was nothing there and then accuse me of deleting

Chapter 2: John 10:10a The Thief

information and just start a fight. I would attempt to fight back at times, but it only got worse, so eventually I gave that up. If I got bold enough to fight, I would get hit even harder, I remember crying so much because of the physical pain I was experiencing. You would think that would make him stop but no, it fueled him up more. It was like he got even stronger and was excited to be able to inflict so much pain on me.

I thank God that I never had a broken bone, but I have had black eyes, busted lips, bite marks, scratches, and bruises all over my body. I was never really a fan of make-up but would have to wear it a lot to cover up the bruises so that people would not stare or ask questions. I also had to wear long sleeves or jackets to cover my arms. I would have to cancel plans with my friends or family because I wasn't in shape to go anywhere. I would look in the mirror and just get disgusted with what I saw sometimes because the image that I saw was not of me and it would bring me to tears.

There were moments when I felt things were getting better and we would be on good terms. We would celebrate holidays with family and friends. We went out of town and hung out, I mean it was like we were turning a new leaf and happiness was coming back into the picture. We were making our house feel like a home. But it didn't last long, it was like he would get ticked off by something so simple and then I was the target. If I voiced my opinion, and it wasn't in his favor, it would cause trouble and I would have to pay for my words. I began to feel like he was the parent, and I was the child.

I knew something was wrong but I couldn't put my finger on it right away, later I found out that drugs were the root cause. I remember cooking dinner one evening and he came home with this nasty attitude and went into the room to take a nap. I guess we had too much noise going for him, so he got up and went to the kitchen and grabbed the pots and just slung them causing the food to go all over the place. I was so upset I just cried because why would you do something like that? My son was right there, and he became upset and went and grabbed a knife but because I knew this could turn ugly, I just calmed him down and sent him into his room. And the enemy packed up his bags and left for the night giving us peace.

I would be tortured in so many ways by this man, but still, I couldn't leave, I really felt like I was trapped. For instance, I would have to walk at least six miles or more home because he wouldn't pick me up from work. He would take my car and leave me stranded many times. I would even be afraid to get in the car with him alone at times because I felt he was going to do something to me. He would drive the car crazily and make me think he was going to crash us. We would go on these back dark, vacant

Chapter 2: John 10:10a The Thief

roads where he would park and make me very afraid.

I couldn't have male friends either because he thought something was going on with them. For instance, I had a friend I was close with since childhood and we always stayed in touch with each other I let him know of this, but anytime this friend called me he would start something with me and even try to argue with the dude. I never cheated or even thought about cheating, but he just kept assuming I was doing something when it was him doing all the wrong. It caused me to draw back from the friendship just because of embarrassment. I know my friend only wanted the best for me, but I just couldn't see or hear clearly.

I would vent to my circle of female friends about what I was dealing with, and we would laugh about it but deep inside I was hurt, afraid, and just confused. I really thought this was the way things were supposed to be. In my mind, I felt like he did love me but just didn't know how to express it except through abuse. I really loved and wanted so desperately to help him. I would continue to hide behind smiles, pictures, and fun moments. I would go to work like everything was normal but inside I was in pain. I lied often when people would try to check on me to see how I was doing.

I started to keep track of some of the abuse and store the pictures in my phone so that I could go back and reflect on them and muster up the courage to leave, but I couldn't do it. The pictures would just make me cry and reveal to him that I was in pain, and it was not right to keep hitting on me. That did nothing though it just caused him to calm down briefly and say he will get better but by this time I knew it wasn't going to happen. He would say whatever needed to be said to keep me near him. Like the time I left home and stayed at someone else's house because of a fight we were in. He called all night crying and texting saying he was going to harm himself if I didn't come back. He put on a good show and eventually, I came back but only because my kids had to return home.

See when my kids were near me, he wouldn't get as aggressive. He would be mad and give me looks, but if they were close by, I was safe. My kids didn't know it, but I used to try to keep them home a lot during this time because it was the only time, I would have peace. I would always invite other kids over and try to keep the house full because that meant he would be gone with his friends, and I would be left alone. However, once everyone left it was back to the basics and I would have to endure whatever may come up.

I suffered these things in silence out of fear of either him hurting himself or me being embarrassed because I loved him and did not want to leave him. I felt that we had a special connection and if I left, I wouldn't be able

Chapter 2: John 10:10a The Thief

to live. It was like he was my lifeline, so I decided I would keep all of this to myself. I never wanted to get anyone involved when I knew I was going right back. I was not ready to leave him, and no one could do anything about it. It would have been a total waste at the time. And I often was asked the question of why I never left or got help and my answer has always been the same, I knew I wasn't done and was going to go right back to the person. There was a deep soul tie that was too tough to break.

I had started going to church more in this season and I was beginning to get tired. I wasn't at the point of leaving but I was getting there. So much was happening, and I was getting drained and felt like there had to be something better for me. The messages at church did not add up to the experiences I was having at home. I think he knew his time was winding down because he began to go into beast mode.

One day he had me upset about something, so I questioned him about it once I got out of the shower and all I remember was waking up on the ground with blood pouring from my face. At this point, I am starting to realize this is bad because I never had to go to a hospital because of domestic violence. They asked what happened but again I lied and said I fell out of the shower. I began to realize the seriousness of this because this incident happened on my daughter's birthday, and I began to wonder if I would live to see another one.

What makes matters worse is that a sister-in-law of mine was murdered by her husband shortly after and he knew the guy. It put this fear in me because just weeks ago she called me to ask me if I was okay and how I was doing, but I had no idea that she was battling or suffering the same thing. My mind began to go into this panic fear mode thinking that I was next on the list. So, I began to walk on eggshells and tried my best not to make him upset. I wanted out and I had to execute a plan that would keep me alive. I was beginning to feel that I had had enough at this point.

After the death of my sister-in-law, I decided that the kids and I would stay at my mom's house for a little until I felt comfortable going back home. Here is where it began to get real, it's hard to talk about because never in my life did, I expect to go through this. I knew I wasn't perfect, and I did my best to be a good woman. I handled all of my responsibilities, took care of my household, attended school, and went to church here and there. I didn't get into a lot of drama like that unless it came to me. I started to see that I was too much for him and he didn't know how to handle someone like me. It was like a light bulb had finally gone off in my head.

So, while staying at my mom's, he would call and text me so much, to the point where I had to just shut the phone

Chapter 2: John 10:10a The Thief

down and not respond. Man, why did I do that? I woke up to at least a hundred missed calls and text messages, but that had nothing on what I was about to walk into when I went home. I unlocked my door and just stood there in tears; my apartment looked like a tornado hit it. Stuff was just everywhere, pictures were ripped, furniture was messed up, and clothes were everywhere, I just could not believe my eyes. I knew then that I could not come back to this place and live a normal life, I had to leave. I wanted this to be as seamless as possible without him going on a tangent.

I told him I could no longer afford the apartment and I just let it go. I had to go and stay with my mom for a while until I felt things had cooled down. It wasn't long before he started coming out to her neighborhood doing stupid things such as honking the horn or revving up the engine to let me know he was outside watching me. It got so aggravating, and my mom was getting annoyed. She knew a little of what was going on but because I did not admit it, she couldn't do much, but she did have a conversation with him, and that calmed him down for a bit. I knew I couldn't hide it much longer because I was staying in her house.

We had two cars, one I purchased and the other he purchased. He had keys to both and would come and take the car I was using so I would have to depend on him for rides whenever I needed to go places. He always tried to find something to hold over me to keep me connected to him. I was miserable and couldn't blame anyone but myself. I had no life at this point but school, work, and church. I didn't feel like doing much else because I would have to ask for a ride or explain where I was going and why, it was just too much. Things were about to change though.

Fast forward a few months, things were calm for a while and we developed somewhat of a friendship, I felt I had to do whatever just to keep peace between us. However, what took place next was the final straw that made me wake up and do something. All it took was this one night when it was a life-or-death matter. He asked me to come to see him after hanging out with my uncle and his girl at this concert, so I asked a mutual friend for a ride. At this time, none of the cars were in my possession and I didn't even care about them.

As I walked into the hotel room the first thing he did was ask to see my phone. So, I'm like, *I know this ain't what I came here for, I'm not doing that.* I was sick of it at this point because we weren't together like that, and he had other relationships or situation-ships that he was involved in. He takes my phone and I just walked out of the room, get back into the car, and use her phone to shut my phone down. I cut off the access so nothing on the

Chapter 2: John 10:10a The Thief

phone worked anymore. I told the girl to take me back home because I was not going back into what I was just getting out of.

He was upset because I was at the concert and concerned if I was talking to other guys, but it should have never been any of his business. I knew in my gut I shouldn't have come here but a part of me still loved him even though I knew he was bad business and I missed him a little. As we approached the entrance to the community where I lived, he was there. We didn't see him leave, so it was mind-boggling as to how he got to the house before I did. But anyways, here we are face to face. He pulls up to the girl's car and tells her to let the window down. I'm telling her no don't do it. He's yelling and screaming making a scene, acting like he has a weapon on his person. I knew he was bluffing because he didn't want to hurt anyone but me. But because he kept making threats, she was afraid and let the window down.

He snatched me right up out of that window and dragged me to the car. I told the girl to call my mom because I knew this wasn't going to end well. He told her not to, but I said if anything happens to me, please call my mom, and let her know what happened. I gave her the number to make sure she knew I was serious. I get in the car and his homeboy is sitting in the passenger seat, mind you he was at the hotel knowing what had taken place already. He told him to drive back to the hotel and I am in the back seat. He began to beat me and hit me so many times I lost count. I just remember blow after blow after blow.

The friend was following us and begged him to pull over and let me out of the car. She made up some lie about how she needed me to do something for her. He wasn't going for it, she begged him repeatedly until he gave in and said I could ride with her, but I had to come back to the hotel. So, I get in the car with her, and he takes over driving but then follows us again and makes us pull back over because he didn't trust her, so I had to get back in the car with him and once we got back to the hotel it was on again.

The girl ended up calling the police and telling them where we were, but they didn't know which room it was. He made me be quiet and he cut the lights off. At this point, I'm held at gunpoint so I can't scream or say anything because the gun is pointed in my direction, and he is sitting there contemplating on what to do. Tears are falling from his eyes, and I'm terrified because I don't know if this will be my last day on this earth. Meanwhile, his friend just sat there watching it all go down, saying nothing.

I remember looking him in the eyes so he could see the hurt in my eyes because this same friend just months

Chapter 2: John 10:10a The Thief

earlier had spoken to me on the side and said he didn't like what was happening to me. He said he would not let anything like that go down around him, but I see when put in the position to defend me he folded. He couldn't even look at me because he knew this was all wrong and that things could go left real quick. I felt so betrayed and confused because my life was on the line and no one was there to help me. The only thing he was good for was removing the gun at the end.

But during this time, I began to reflect on my life and all that I have been through, and for it to come to this I was like *WOW*. I did not want this to be the end of my story. I had to find a way out of this, *Lord God please don't let me die*. My kids need me and I need them. Let this not be the end. These are the thoughts going through my head. I began to pray and repent of my sins. I also tried to talk my way out of this saying that this is not what you want to do because it won't end well for the both of us. I told him to think about my children and my family.

That night I made my mind up that I was done with this man and made a vow to leave him alone for good. It was time to let go and move forward. I have never in my life experienced this type of abuse that I went through. I was okay with a push, a shove, or a punch, but the torture I experienced in different ways was just way too much to bear. I was beaten for hours and felt so helpless. The people around me couldn't help me; only God could. I was saved by a phone call from my mom and grandma. (God heard my prayer).

The cycle of abuse I found myself in was pure torture. I found myself going deeper and deeper into this hole that I could not escape. I wanted to get out, but I just didn't know how because it began to feel like home, and I felt I just couldn't give up so easily. I wanted things to change desperately, and I really thought they would. I mean I prayed and asked God to change the situation and to make it better. I shed blood, sweat, and tears for this relationship so in my mind it just had to work.

I never knew that someone who loved me could beat me as badly as they did that night. And to top it off, I didn't even do anything to deserve it. All I ever did was love him with every bone in my body. But once God spared my life, I was done… the next day I went and filed a police report and had a restraining order issued. I had to protect myself. Enough was finally enough for me.

CHAPTER 3:
JOHN 10:10B THE LIFEGIVER

We all know what the thief had set out to do in my life, but if you keep reading that same passage of scripture it ends with:

> *I came that they may have life, and have it in abundance [to the full, till it overflows].*
> **John 10:10b (AMP)**

You may be saying, "Man, he really had it in for her, I'm surprised that she is even here today to be able to share her story." My reply to you is, "Yes, he had devised this great, big plan to take me out. He knew all the components and key people to use for his plan and was ready to execute." However, there was One sitting high and looking low, waiting for the exact moment and time to come in and give me something that only He could provide. Had I not called His name and asked Him to save me the story could have ended abruptly right there. But He had greater plans in store for me that the darkness tried to blind and keep me trapped from.

Life was waiting on the other side of the tunnel. Even though I could not see it at the time, it was nearby, I just had to make it to the other side. I was a willing participant in this darkness and did not know I was killing myself spiritually until the Life-giver came and intervened. He was not done with me and had a plan and purpose for my life. Yes, the enemy had a plan for me, but my God said, "No." The one who gives life is above the one who comes to steal, kill, and destroy.

I never realized how God was with me throughout my entire life and was sustaining me along the way. Every event that was set as a trap to cause my demise actually made me stronger. I never understood why I had this drive to just keep moving forward no matter how hard it got. I wanted to throw in the towel many times, but something just would not let me. Come to find out, years later it was Him all along. He needed me here on this earth. He knew that my story resembled a lot of others and that they could witness Him and have the same encounter that I had.

That is why He would send people into my life that would try to help me along the way such as coworkers, bosses, and even strangers. For instance, there was a girl I knew through a mutual contact, she was not my friend

Chapter 3: John 10:10b The Lifegiver

at the time. She approached me one day and let me know that she knew what was going on. She saw through the makeup and wanted me to be honest and real about what I was experiencing. She wanted me to know that she cared and was there for me, along with her family. I was embarrassed at first but one day she popped up to my house and asked me if I wanted to go walking, I agreed. As we walked and talked, she explained to me how she too experienced this and that I didn't deserve it.

She didn't judge me or make me feel bad for being in the situation I was in; she was just concerned. She was a shoulder that I could lean on, but because I was living in fear I continued to stay. She told me to fight back and protect myself and I told her that I did but it didn't help any, it just got worse. She and her family became a safe haven for me during my domestic abuse. They would just pour into me and encourage me to do better. I valued what they said and tried to do for me but because of fear I stayed put.

I think God for her though because, unlike the friends that I was surrounded by, she called me out on my truth and saw there was a problem. She became a real friend to me and walked with me through my pain. She believed in me and was always available to talk when I needed her. After all those years she was able to witness me on my road to redemption and see the hand of God upon my life.

God knew who I needed to have in my life at the right moments.

There have been many cases known and I'm sure unknown where death was knocking but God blocked it. I had suffered two ectopic pregnancies, where I was once told that I died and had to be brought back and the other I got to the hospital in the nick of time. I had very bad nearly tragic car accidents: 1) hit an 18-wheeler on I-95, did a couple of donuts and latched on to the truck, and was drug a few miles, 2) rear-ended by a truck going up the overpass to merge onto I-95 and flipping over the ramp at least five times down a hill, and 3) being T-boned by a driver on their cellphone. And guess what? I was with "him" in all these situations.

Facing death by being in abusive relationships, suicide attempts, using drugs, taking charges, financial dilemmas, health risks, and so many other things could have been the end of my story. I mean so many nights I would lay in bed and just ask God to let me die. I begged Him to not let me wake up from my sleep sometimes because life was just too hard for me. But because of Jesus, none of those things became my reality. He really was the Life-giver and wanted me to experience a full life with no limits. He knew something better than I knew and was not going to allow me to just give up so easily.

What I saw as a dead end, He saw as a new beginning.

Chapter 3: John 10:10b The Lifegiver

Without Him, life was not worth living and the thief was able to just run wild in my life doing whatever he could to break me down. Look at each near-death experience I faced and how what was meant to kill me only made me stronger. I was able to walk away from those accidents with little to no injuries. I was able to walk out of those hospitals after having emergency surgery. I was able to stop using drugs immediately without any side effects or addictions overcoming me. I was able to walk away from death and into eternal life all because of the Life-giver.

My transition to life was not easy either, so let me just tell you this now. There were many times when I made mistakes and even backtracked and danced with the enemy out of habit and comfort. But because I was introduced to the Life-giver, I no longer had to face those things alone. I now had someone to walk with me, lead me, and guide me along the way. When I stumbled and fell, He did not talk badly about me or treat me indifferently, He loved me and helped me get to where He needed me to be. I was able to learn to trust Him and not man. The enemy's grip began to loosen as I grabbed hold of Him. He began to show me the life He had for me waiting ahead if I would fully surrender to Him.

He saw everything I was and had become and took me through a process of redemption. He knew that I needed to be free and clear of some things in order to receive what He had for me. The journey to this abundant life was life-changing, there was a lot of silence at first but over time there was a shift, and His voice became clear.

CHAPTER 4:
SEPARATION

Separation? Who me? How does one do this? For anyone who has been in relationship after relationship and has always been surrounded by people, what exactly does separation look like? Can you really detach yourself from everyone and spend time alone? Do you even have the boldness to step away from everything you have known and become accustomed to? These are the questions one would think about when being called into unfamiliar territory.

God needed me to get away from the norm so that we could get to know each other on a more personal, intimate level. I was desperate to escape and just be alone with all that I just went through. I had this paranoid feeling that had me looking at everyone as a suspect. I couldn't tell who was for me or against me. I was not comfortable, I felt stares and heard rumors that people would speak about me. So, when separation came, I welcomed it with open arms.

I immediately began blocking phone numbers and screening calls. I shut down everything and focused on school, work, and my children. I had no time for anything that would not be beneficial to me. I even gave up my social media platforms. I didn't want to see anyone or anything that would trigger me. I was happy to be alive and back home after a traumatic event. But I was living in fear and only God could help me.

Only a couple of people knew what I had just experienced, so being silent and unseen was the best thing for me. I was lost, my spirit was grieved, and my soul was aching. I wasn't in the best mood when it came to fellowshipping and being around people. Which is crazy because I was used to being the life of the party and always surrounded by people. But I needed time to process it all because at the core my heart was still with him. I felt the people in my life at the time would only want to be nosey and get information.

I didn't think they cared about me; I would have been just another girl on a t-shirt with a hashtag. That's usually what's done when a person dies due to violence. They promote your death and try to find out what happened, but not to address the issues or make things better but more so to be nosey and gossip. So, I began to distance myself from a lot of people. I became less and less available

Chapter 4: Separation

intentionally.

I knew I needed a real change, but I wasn't so sure as to where to start. I knew I didn't want the input of others and it needed to be done alone. I had some soul-searching and rediscovering to do. I needed to find Ashle' because I had gotten so lost and out of tune with my true self. My life consisted of catering to others and their needs. I didn't do too much outside of my home unless I was with him. I was on his timetable and had to work around his schedule. Nothing was being poured into me, I was empty.

I needed to face myself in the mirror and tell the truth. I was torn, beaten, and shattered. I was afraid and I needed help. And truth be told, I didn't feel I had anyone that I could go to that would fully understand how I could still love "him" despite what he did. No one was able to understand how mentally I was battling depression, low self-esteem, anger, resentment, suicidal thoughts, grief, loneliness, rejection, neglect and so much more all at one time.

About this time, I began to realize that a fear of men gripped me and caused me to look at every man as "him." I wanted to be invisible to them and didn't want to be bothered. If I saw a man on the same side of the street as me, I would cross the street. If they spoke, I would hold my head down or act as if I didn't hear them. I was in a paranoid state and no man was safe unless I already knew you. My trust had been messed up and I really was not okay, but I couldn't force myself to say it just yet.

I would speak less and just kind of like ghost people because I didn't want to talk. I did not want to explain what I had been dealing with because I did not know exactly what to call it. So, I did the best thing I could and that was to withdraw. To make it make sense, it was like, I was in a room full of people but felt awkward, sort of like an outcast if I am honest, I didn't feel like I fit in anymore. The people didn't do anything to make me feel this way I was just in another place in life and wanted to be invisible. And to any man that I may have offended along the way due to my trauma, let me pause right here and say, "I sincerely apologize, I never meant to offend you, I was just going through some things and didn't know how to handle it."

I had been to church for most of my life and I knew about Jesus, I mean I did attend private school and participated in the Chapel services, so I knew many verses of scripture by heart. I knew what it meant to have a relationship with Jesus too, I just never really pursued one or got to really know Him for myself on a more intimate level. But after praying and asking for my life to be spared it was only right, I began to work on this relationship. I started attending a local church in my area, away from family and friends. I needed to go to a place where no

Chapter 4: Separation

one knew me so that I wouldn't be influenced by others. I needed a fresh start and why not with Christ Fellowship Church, it was diverse and had many campuses with a lot of attendees.

I also started reading the Bible and guess where I was led to start... The Book of Revelation. In hindsight, I know now it was nothing but the Holy Spirit who led me there. He knew what I needed to get the ball rolling. After reading Revelation, I looked at my life and was like, *if I die today, I think I'm going to hell.* I had been shacking up, fornicating, using profanity, and living the opposite of a righteous life. I considered myself a lukewarm Christian, so I knew it was time to get my life right.

My passion for reading had never left me, what a blessing. It actually grew in this season, and I found myself reading so many different books of the Bible including books regarding prayer, faith, dating, and all things kingdom. I would do devotionals and Bible study books that would help deepen my faith walk. I was hungry and thirsty for the Lord. I felt I had to make up for lost time and catch up on so much. The funny thing is God wasn't in a rush, but I needed to do whatever I felt it took to help me get over my pain. I now had something and Someone to turn to that was not a drug or human being that would take advantage.

I was learning so much about myself through the word

of God and those other books that I didn't have time for anything else. I recall reading *The New Rules for Love, Sex, & Dating* by Andy Stanley and he was talking about how after a breakup it would be good to spend at least a year alone to unpack the baggage of the relationship and get to know yourself (2014). Until reading that I never thought about this period of separation being a blessing. I was used to going from man to man and taking all my baggage from the previous relationship into the next one. I took the advice of this book and not only did it with men but with everyone. I needed alone time away from family and friends too. There were too many like-minded people in my life dealing with similar issues and I needed a new scene.

I set up a schedule where I would have personal intimacy with God in the morning and evening. I created a prayer wall and had sticky notes and cards of people that I would pray for. I would post notes around the house with verses of scripture so that I could recite the verse every time I saw it. I was learning how to develop discipline and be committed to my time with the Lord. I would sometimes fall asleep praying on the floor in my prayer corner in my room. I also included my children in my prayer time. We had established a nighttime routine where we would pray before bed as a family and take turns each night.

I also started to fast so that I could meet God in a

Chapter 4: Separation

more intimate secret place. This was a new experience but something that I had longed for. I never knew the true power of praying and fasting until I did it myself. I had to give up the things that I was used to, to be able to get results that I never had before. I was able to experience God in a new way. There was a deeper connection, and I was able to feel safe and more secure. He was there and willing to listen all the time.

Fasting was new for me and man, let me tell you lol my first fast was hilarious. I mean at the time it wasn't but now I can laugh because I did not know what I was fully getting into, but I had the right heart. I was doing the "Daniel" fast, which eliminates all meats, sweets, and treats. I tried to prepare and get all the right food items in advance, but found myself with bad headaches and hunger pangs out of this world. I was already skinny due to poor eating habits from all the trauma I had recently experienced. So, my fasting was just like an accident waiting to happen. I checked the scale one day and I was 90 lbs. lol...my kids were bigger than me it was sad, and my ribs were nearly showing. Can you begin to imagine what was being said about me...all I can say is OMG, thank God for separation.

Long story short, I had some powerful breakthroughs during this time. I was building with the Lord and He began to show me favor in so many different ways. Doors were opening and closing for me where needed. Fasting had been a door opener to the true power of God in my life. I was separated from the world and was focusing more on the Lord. It was like the Lord knew that I would be facing some tough decisions ahead and I needed His strength to overcome them.

I had some deep soul ties that needed to be broken along with some deep wounds that needed healing. Time was on my side and the Lord began to reveal to me the spiritual aspect of things. It wasn't the people, but the spirit attached to the people and operating through them that was the problem. I was not to hate the person or mistreat them but forgive them because they didn't know what they were doing. I started a forgiveness journey and began forgiving each person that was used in my life to hurt me. I prayed for them and their souls. I wanted God to bless them and change them as He was changing me. I wanted them to experience what I had. I was reminded of Jesus and the character He displayed as He was being led to the cross. I had taken on that same heart as my Lord. I started journaling and writing prayers. I had to personally forgive each person who did me harm and release them of their offense, from my youth to adulthood. And then I had to do the BIG one eventually….

I had to forgive myself for the abuse I put myself through. No one forced me to start or stay in those

Chapter 4: Separation

relationships, it was out of my own free will. Also, my choosing to date guys back-to-back and live a promiscuous life was on me. I was lost and looking for love that no one could actually give me. I wanted to desperately fit in with the crowds and be the chick with all the attention, but it was for all the wrong reasons. I did a lot of things that I shouldn't have done to my body, but I had to be woman enough to admit to myself that I was an abuser to myself just like the others were.

Separation is needed in different seasons of life, and I want you to know that it is okay to be separated for a while. On this journey, you gain self-confidence and love that you never thought you were missing. We never really know and understand who we truly are if we are always surrounded by people. Jesus is the perfect example when it comes to separation. He went away many times to pray and gain strength so we too must follow and take the lead. Some may understand and some may not fully get it and that is ok. But if God is calling you to take a step back and separate, do it because I am telling you now if I had not, I don't know where I would be. Ministry, joy, peace, self-control, kindness, forgiveness, love, wisdom, wholeness, new relationships and so much more was birthed in my separation.

I later started attending Life Groups that my local church was having with a diverse group of women.

New relationships were beginning to be formed with no prejudgment or preconceived notions. I even surprised myself by volunteering and serving on Saturdays and Sundays with the church. I was becoming someone I never knew I could be; the real light was starting to show. Being able to help others and meet new people from all walks of life was a breath of fresh air to me. And the one common ground that brought us together was: Jesus.

Most people I knew didn't understand how I could go through what I experienced and still end up where I am today. But God had a plan for me that I fully didn't understand myself. He would send people into my path to help me along the way. These people were strangers that became close to me. People who genuinely loved and cared about me. They helped me to see myself in the image of God, encouraged me, and helped build me up. And if I had never taken that time away with Him, I would have probably missed these things.

I later was released to have friends again and would find myself inviting people to church and seeing how I could serve them. I even reconnected with my family because I needed them too. It was all done in moderation though because I was still fragile and didn't trust everyone as I did before. And even though we may have to be called into separation, we are still not to do life alone permanently.

CHAPTER 5:
DO YOU SEE WHAT I SEE?

We all have an image of ourselves and what we see when we look in the mirror. Some feel good about themselves and have confidence while others may feel down and suffer from low self-esteem. Depending on your upbringing and environment would have a lot to do with how you view yourself. Society also has standards and then we fall into this comparison trap and find or should I say look for value in things, people, success, and accomplishments. But below the surface, it's deeper than that. We desperately want to fit in with the culture and seem cool to the world.

I don't know about you, but as you have read in a previous chapter, I lived to seek attention. I wanted to be seen and known as the cool down to earth chick. I wanted to boast about my loyalty and the good attributes that I brought to the table. I wanted people to see the good in me and just love me. The problem with this is that it was always centered around people. So, when they would reject me or treat me badly it would tear me up on the inside and cause me to feel low and unworthy. I was fighting a never-ending battle.

The opinions of others mattered so much and when I tried to overcome it and act like it wasn't a big deal it brought on more pain and confusion. I lost myself and didn't have an identity. I knew I possessed good qualities and attributes, but I was not as confident in them anymore. I never really saw myself as who God created me to be. It was more so of what people expected me to be. I didn't pay attention to my Creator nor His word. I didn't look at myself through His lens. I did not even know that He cared for me as much as He did until I hit rock bottom and was facing death.

I was so used to being who others wanted me to be that I never took the time to truly know who I was. I would often look into the mirror and get aggravated because I felt I never measured up to what society called beautiful. I didn't see myself as a good dresser, I would just put stuff together hoping it looked right. I had no true identity and I always wanted to get approval from others when it came to style. I felt I had no taste, and I would be picked on because of what I chose to wear. I didn't do makeup as

Chapter 5: Do You See What I See?

much and when I did it was simple, not too in-depth, just something to keep up with everyone else.

One day, the Lord spoke to me and called me to the mirror and had me to really look at myself. Not in the physical but in the spiritual and that's when it clicked. I noticed that I was beautiful. He told me that I was beautiful inside and that it was reflected on the outside. He let me know that people did not see what He saw in me. God saw the real me at my core, the me that I desperately wanted people to see, He saw that. He saw that my soul was beautiful and though I had made some poor decisions, I was someone that He could use.

He began to minister to me and build me up and I was able to learn that the world had no hold on me when it came to my true beauty. He revealed that I was the apple of His eye, and no one would be able to take the love that He has for me away. My identity was found in Him. He was the one who created me and made me to be one of a kind. I struggled with trying to find out how I could be the only one who felt the ways that I felt and did the things that I did but as time went on, I began to see I was not the only one.

I loved people and had the desire to help those in need, I still do now. My actions displayed the characteristics of God. When people misused and abused me, I did not treat them as they treated me, I still loved them and treated them fairly. I had a servant's heart and would be a loyal person to whomever I encountered. I loved children that weren't mine and took care of them. I didn't let what I went through change my true nature as a nurturer. I may have not fully understood His character and may have misused them many times, but He was teaching me and training me how to be more like Him.

I began to see myself in a new light and I vowed to allow that light to shine no matter the circumstances. God saw things in me that had been suppressed and held back because of others. There was a boldness and uniqueness in me. As I developed and built these characters, I began to hold my head high, and I noticed my outward appearance began to change. I would often look in the mirror and tell myself that I am beautiful. I smiled more and had confidence in myself that I never knew existed. I wasn't cocky or anything, I just began to see clearly who I was and whose I was.

I was somebody and no one was going to tell me any different. I began to speak up for myself and even others. God was doing work in me, and He wanted me to come from behind the veil. Fear and intimidation had to go, as it was no longer my portion, I was fearfully and wonderfully made by God, and I had a destiny to fulfill. I was beginning to see what He saw in me. He saw greatness, humility, and authenticity along with a host of other things, but most

Chapter 5: Do You See What I See?

importantly He saw my heart. Like David, I became a woman after God's own heart. I was not perfect, and I made many mistakes, but I didn't let it take away from the fact that I was a changed woman.

I came to God broken in heart and spirit. I was lost and did not fully know which way to go. I felt I did everything I was supposed to do to be an honest woman. I loved hard and made many sacrifices for others. I had talent and beauty to offer, I was not some dull female without goals, dreams, or aspirations. I had visions and plans and I worked towards them all. I was a strong independent woman according to the standard of the world because I had my own place, car, and job. I took care of grown men and their children. I mean what else was there to do?

With all that mentioned, it meant nothing because there was no identity behind it. There was so much still missing and what God knew I truly needed to complete me was His Son. I needed a Savior. Someone who would take what I had and use it to bring glory to Him. I was operating in my own strength, but He saw that I was weak and tired, He saw that I was in need of help. I was getting beat down constantly by trying to measure up and fit many shoes.

He saw my future and where I was headed if I did not come to Him for help. God was looking at the internal while man only saw the external. So, when I came to Him fully and surrendered myself to Him, I was able to walk away a new creature. The old things had passed away and all things had become new for me. I was finally able to see the inner me which then helped form the outer me. God didn't want me to live a life according to the world's standards, but according to His Kingdom's standards.

And even to this day, I made that my mission, to live a life devoted to Him and not the world. Anytime I find myself getting sucked into the way the world views or sees things I withdraw and go into a secret place with God to rebuild my confidence and self-esteem. I went as far as getting a tattoo on my chest stating "I am enough" to remind me of who I am and that my identity is not found in man. I love myself now because I understand who I am. I was at a very low and sunken place but because I gave Him a try, everything has turned around for my good and His glory.

CHAPTER 6:
R&R (REBUILD & RESTORE)

How does one go from losing just about everything they have to gaining it all back and some within a matter of years? The only answer I can honestly give you is God. He knew my struggles and saw everything I had been stripped of. He witnessed the sleepless nights, the crying, the worry, the doubt, and so forth. If anyone knew my pain it was Him. So, I just have to stop and humbly say *thank God for Jesus* because I don't look like, nor smell like, what I have been through. My Apostle said in a sermon one time that, "God didn't let you die because you had a destiny to fulfill." What a profound and powerful statement to make. I mean looking at all I had been through; I was able to finally understand why God did not allow the enemy to kill me.

The enemy took all that I had worked hard to gain

such as my car, my apartment, my money, my identity, my friends, and so much more. But what he didn't know was that God was working behind the scenes. And every area that the enemy touched was about to get restored in due time. God was going to have the final say over my life and get all the glory that He so rightly deserved. How I see it is that without those life-altering experiences, there would be no testimony or story to tell. So, I'm going to use this chapter to "Brag on my Lord" as Christian Artist Trip Lee says in one of his songs.

I know I may look young, but I have wisdom beyond my years. What I have learned is that in order for God to truly bless you and restore you He has to have your heart and full commitment. God is not to be treated as a genie in a bottle or someone who you can give a little to gain a lot. So, as I tell you what He did for me, know that it came after I fully surrendered and gave my life to Him. I did not hold anything back. I had to let go of what I was used to completely. I had to cut some people off and turn down things that I knew my flesh loved. I had to take a stand and do what was right according to His Word. It took discipline, humility, and commitment. I stumbled a couple of times because it was all new to me, but God didn't give up on me. He knew what I was ready for and when I was ready for it. As the saying goes, "He may not come when you want it, but He will be there right on time."

Chapter 6: R&R (Rebuild & Restore)

God knows your real heart and He will not just give you something that He knows would harm you. He has to know that you are ready and able to manage what He gives you. God is not like man where you just say that you are ready, He has to see it. He sees what man does not see. You have to be committed to Him in public and in private. Everything isn't always glittery, there is work that is required. There is a new Kingdom standard that we have to get accustomed to.

I now understand the passage in the book of James when he says to count it all joy when you fall into divers temptations (James 1:2, KJV). Because in life you will have some tests and temptations that come up unexpectedly. The enemy presented himself to me in a way that seemed irresistible. In my own understanding, I just knew how everything was going to go and had life all figured out. Only to wake up and realize I was just a pawn in the hands of the enemy. He laid out the road map of destruction before me and I was just blindly walking the course.

Despite the start of the journey and how it looked, God had His hands on me from start to finish. I feel like I was specifically chosen for these assignments because He knew my heart and how I would handle these situations. Most people wouldn't be able to walk a mile in my shoes let alone even share what I am sharing out of fear of what the world may think or say, they would have been threw in the towel. And I wouldn't blame them either because many times that is what I wanted to do but Holy Spirit said, "Nope, keep fighting," and that's exactly what I did.

Every test, trial, tribulation, and experience taught me how to really depend on Him no matter what. I remember reading scripture and being like *dang, these people went through it.* I was happy they paved the way too, but not knowing my own story was being written as I was reading theirs. But we know God is funny and works in mysterious ways, so it comes with the territory. He let me see the good and the bad. I saw life without God and life with God and let's just say, I picked a side because, baby, the world doesn't love nobody!

The first thing He began working on was my emotional healing. I was no longer able to be controlled, manipulated, or mishandled as before. It was new so of course people thought I was acting "brand new" or too high and mighty, but truth be told I had come into my true identity and gained some confidence. The enemy had been served his notice that his time was up and whatever he wanted to do to me should have been done when he had the chance. God showed me how to be me but in a godly, wholesome, righteous way. I was able to have fun and enjoy life doing the things I loved and being around the people I loved. I just established boundaries this time.

Chapter 6: R&R (Rebuild & Restore)

I learned to not allow my feelings to dictate how I responded to others. I was able to control my surroundings and what I would and would not allow. I had plans in place in case I ever felt uncomfortable and needed to leave. People were going to be people and just because they had a different view from mine didn't make them right. I did my best to avoid negative conversations and kept people on a need-to-know basis. I did talk about my walk with Christ though and shared how He changed my life; I mean what person would keep this newfound love to themselves? There was something different about me and they could tell.

Low self-esteem became a thing of the past. I had a voice and wasn't afraid to use it. You know the "uncircumcised Philistine" tried to come and show his head a few times, but I had to remind him of what thus says the Lord. And yea that's my nickname for the devil because he was like a Goliath to me all bark but no bite when it came to God Almighty. My validation no longer came from people and if anyone tried to get in my way, I would disconnect myself quickly. Now, I'm not saying all people are bad and meant harm, but what I am saying is that those who had a negative impact and were not filled with Holy Spirit had no say so over my life and limited access to me.

I began to stand up for myself more often, as people

were more so used to the old quiet, naïve Ashle'. I deserved respect and to be taken seriously just like everyone else. I was no longer a child. I did not just go with the flow of things; I had my own mind and made my own decisions. My values and beliefs had changed so when things would happen that did not line up, I would address it in a godly fashion. I no longer took offense or held grudges against others because they did something I didn't agree with. I would just remove myself and apologize if needed.

Emotionally God had rebuilt His identity in me and restored my self-esteem. He made it to where I did not allow others to run over me and I didn't take a lot of stuff personally. I stayed in the word and kept digging deeper when it came to the things of God. This rubbed off into my relational healing, which really shocked me lol because I had thought in my mind, I would never trust anyone let alone get close to another person. I only cared about my kids at this point and my relationship with God. But slowly God was removing the wall that I built, unbeknownst to me. As I fell in love with God, He began to show me how my children were just like I was. They were innocent and didn't ask to be here. They were blessings given to me by Him, even though I had them out of wedlock.

The love He gave me was the same love I was expected to give to them. My children didn't see everything I went through, but they felt it. The chaos that surrounded

Chapter 6: R&R (Rebuild & Restore)

them was traumatizing and not fair. Because I chose to be in those relationships it caused a major strain on the relationship we had. I wasn't fully in my right mind and put their emotions and feelings on the back burner. I was all for myself. I loved them and cared for them, but I did not take care of them in the way I should have by having them in toxic environments.

I made them out to be liars because when they would tell someone what was going on I would often say it is not true and then get on their case about telling my business to other people. Imagine how they must have felt trying to save their mom but she didn't want to be saved at the time. They started being rebellious at home and school. They would want to leave the house but also be fearful to leave me alone because they knew things weren't right. It would hurt me because I knew my choices were the reason behind it. They had put up with a lot of craziness just to make me happy, but there came a time when they were honest with me and told me they were fed up.

When God delivered me from the abuse things began to turn around, and my relationship with my children was restored. We formed this bond like no other. They embraced the fact that they had their mom back. They were happy and loved to be home. We spent so much time together and had many outings just recreating and creating new memories. We were able to talk about what I went through to a certain extent and how they were feeling in those moments. I was able to apologize to my children and love on them and ensure them that the former life was truly over. I never wanted them to hurt the way they did or experience that again.

We were the Three Musketeers (a term we used when it came to our family). We cooked together, watched movies and TV shows, and just sat around dancing and joking around together sometimes 'til 3-4 in the morning. I saw a different side of my children that I missed so badly but never knew I was missing it. We attended church together and started serving together as a family. Life was great, of course, there were little bumps along the way but from what we had come from it was an upgrade. I was able to be a real parent now and the division that we once experienced due to my abusive relationships no longer existed. God knew that my family needed this reconciliation. Trust was rebuilt and love was restored.

I tried to prevent and hide a lot from them but come to find out they knew more than I thought. They paid attention and were looking and listening when I thought they weren't. Now here is where I want to pause and share something dear to me with parents and caretakers who find themselves in abusive relationships. Whether you thought about it or not, please take the time to consider what I have to say because I wish I had this mindset back

Chapter 6: R&R (Rebuild & Restore)

then.

We have to listen to our children and pay attention to the signs they display when something is going on. Years after the abuse one of my children had a conversation with me and expressed to me how they were still healing from my trauma. I never knew my situation affected them that deeply because it was happening to me. It shocked and blew my mind at the same time because here we are years later, and they felt safe enough to come and let me know that they still were experiencing the effects. I'm not saying to let your children have control over who you date or the decisions you make, but I am saying to take heed and consider them when making life-altering decisions. We have to realize that we as parents are our children's first teachers. Everything they learn first comes from us and follows them into the real world. So, depending on what is being taught in the home could be good or bad. Children learn by action and not by words. Which is why we are to be doers and not just hearers.

I've seen firsthand how children will lose respect for their parents because of abuse and then begin to feel like they can do what others do to their parents. They talk back and begin to be disrespectful toward you. They don't see you as a person in authority but as someone, they can walk over and mistreat. They don't value you or your words anymore, they just brush you off. They even become embarrassed to be around you because they know what people are saying, so it puts them in a compromising position.

If you are in or know someone in a bad relationship and there are children involved, please consider ending that relationship immediately. Kids will think that is the norm and possibly end up being in an abusive relationship. It can affect their mental health and cause emotional trauma in the future. I know you're thinking, *Girl hush, you ain't no therapist* and you're right, I'm not. But what I can say is that I am experienced, and I have witnessed so many people in these situations stay, and their kids go through torture. I saw abuse growing up and look at what happened to me. Let's not make our children suffer and let's not expose them to things that could affect them negatively. We have to think of them and not just ourselves.

After the relationship with my children was restored, I was released to begin restoring certain relationships. So, once God had me forgive all those who wronged me, I begin going to therapy and working on how to interact with those same people in the future. I witnessed how they went through challenging times and suffered the consequences of their actions because of how they mistreated me. I didn't have the heart to be nasty toward them, instead I was able to be cordial, pray for, and even attend church with some of them.

Chapter 6: R&R (Rebuild & Restore)

God needed me to mend those broken relationships so that I would not leave any doors open for the enemy to try and creep in again. I had to fully let go of that hurt and pain, that didn't mean to forget what I went through so I could repeat the same mistakes but more so don't hold on to the past to use it against someone. I wasn't allowed to just pray and forgive them, I had to actually have some conversations. Now, this may be different for you, and I would never tell anyone to contact someone who's not safe to contact. This is just what the Lord led me to do. Those people reached out to me, and I was able to have that talk, I didn't go looking for them to give them a piece of my mind. So please be cautious of things like that.

Sometime later, I realized that my fear of men had gone away because I found myself being interactive and engaging in conversations that I usually would have stayed away from. By me being active in church and volunteering as a greeter, I had to face many people with warm welcoming smiles. I was able to see that all men were not the same and there were no hidden agendas with every person I met. The Lord revealed to me that it was okay to love again in a healthy, godly way but only when the time was right. I wasn't to force anything or allow anyone to persuade me into something I knew I wasn't ready for.

Okay, so now I'm doing a lot better mentally, physically,

and emotionally. I'm healthy I gained my weight back and just getting on my feet. I had the same job, which I am so grateful I didn't lose. I was close to getting fired at least two times that I can remember because I was missing a lot of days and my performance was not the best. But you know God had His hand in that area too, I would apply for promotions over and over, get the interview and do well but not get offered the position. I was stagnated and in a standstill position. I was good at what I did but because of what I was going through it reflected poorly on me.

But here is where it all changed for me in the area of finances. The judge had ruled and because of all the pain and suffering, I was about to get my restitution. See money is a tool that we all need in order to live in this world. We are not to love the money but use the money for the things we need. Remember how I was struggling financially living paycheck to paycheck, my bank account always in the negative, getting evicted and even having repossessions of my car? I was all jacked up with little to no hope.

Well, let me tell you how God showed out on my behalf. It started shortly after I started attending the new church. There was a card in the seat in front of me with the words 310 challenge on it, it was based on Malachi 3:10 (go read that right quick, if you are not familiar with it). The church was willing to refund you one hundred

Chapter 6: R&R (Rebuild & Restore)

percent of your tithes if God did not show up for you in three months. Now this didn't mean just financially it was regarding anything. So, me being in the state I was in I said, "Okay God, I'm going to do this challenge," but I was not about to request my money back I knew better, I just needed something to hold me accountable when it came to my giving.

Before then I had never been a consistent giver. I would just give a few dollars here or there and keep it moving. I knew I was supposed to tithe, but I felt I could not afford to tithe anything because I was always in the negative and didn't have enough money to pay for all the necessities. However, I just decided to give it a try because I'm like what's the worst that could happen? Let's just say, I am so glad that I made that decision and I have been tithing ever since.

I ended up living with my mom for a while after my last eviction, I had no car and had to depend on a friend to drive me around everywhere or I asked my mom to use her car. I had let the other one I shared with "him" go back as a voluntary repo. I wanted nothing to do with it because it always caused an issue with him. The first thing God blessed me with was a car. I found an old used car for sale while driving around and it ran good just didn't have any heat, but hey, I was in need so I purchased it for $600. Next, I began looking for a place for me and my kids to stay because it had been some time since I heard from "him" and guess what… I found this 3-bedroom 1-bath house that was close to my job for $950 a month. I spoke with the landlord and worked out a schedule with him to ensure my payments would be made on time to prevent any further evictions. I also was granted funds from my church and a local program in the neighborhood to pay my first, last, & security deposit. It wasn't the best neighborhood but for the price and location, it was a win-win for the time being.

The kids and I had a place to call our own again. The house was newly renovated and we were the first ones to be able to move in. Everyone had a room of their own and space to do whatever they needed to do without feeling too clustered. I was able to pay my landlord every two weeks for my rent. We were happy and very comfortable in our new place. Plus, to find a place for that cheap of rent was a blessing because I think three-bedrooms were renting from anywhere close to $1,200-$1,500 a month, which I could not have afforded at the time.

Later, down the line, someone from the church gave me a scholarship reward to take the Financial Peace University Course offered by Dave Ramsey (if you don't know who he is or what I am talking about research it, it changed my life). Taking that course helped me to learn so much about my money and how to make it work for me that I immediately began applying the principles to my financial life. I got an accountability partner and saved up my first $1,000 in no time. That was big for me because I never was able to save money, but God made a way for me. Overtime was being offered at the job and I took it and there you have it- $1000 saved. In addition to that I started tithing off of my gross income after reading Robert Morris's book, *The Blessed Life* (read that when you get a chance and thank me later).

Over time, I was getting blessed left and right. I started receiving unexpected deposits into my bank account for money that was owed to me. I would get gift cards in the mail from my local church and even have some friends and family reach out to me to offer me food and groceries without me having to say anything. It was awesome because God really did know my needs and provided for me without me having to even ask. So that passage of scripture in Matthew 6 was becoming alive to me and helping me to see who God really was.

There had been times when I didn't have enough food in the house for us to eat, but I wouldn't complain or tell anyone. I had a little pride and didn't want to feel needy so I just trusted in God and knew that if anything I would just let the kids eat. But once I would get home and check the mail there would be gift cards or I would get a call from someone saying they had something for me. When

I would come over, they would give me money to go get groceries or take me to the store so I could get some food. There were times when people overcooked and had some extra food and dropped it by the house. I would be in tears some nights just thanking God because these people did not truly know how they were being used by Him.

The more God revealed Himself to me the more I desired to be with Him and learn from Him. It didn't mean that I was perfect but it meant I had a foundation and a source to turn to when I drifted and got off track. I remember doing a Bible Study by Priscilla Shirer called "The Full Armor of God." I learned how to really pray and cover not just myself but also my children. I learned how to not be afraid of the enemy and his tricks. I learned that every day I had to be ready and equipped for battle. And bless God for exposing me to this because later I would need it when I was face-to-face with "him" unexpectedly.

So, let me take you back a little bit, let's say a couple months after the restraining order was filed. I didn't see him for a while, and I was okay with that because I thought he had left me alone for good and everything was over. But come to find out he was stalking me unknowingly; he knew where my kids attended school so he would be in an unmarked car watching to see when I would drop them off. He didn't know what kind of car I drove right away and also didn't know my whereabouts so he just

Chapter 6: R&R (Rebuild & Restore)

posted up around the school areas. One day, I noticed a car following me and switching lanes to stay near me. I began to get into different lanes to make sure my mind wasn't playing tricks on me and sure enough they got in the lanes too. I started to pray because I didn't know who this was and what they were trying to do.

Eventually, the car pulled up on the side of me and they rolled down the window and to my surprise, it was "him." Fear gripped me, and I was thinking he came back to finish me. I was not ready for this. He kept asking me to pull over and was laughing, I shook my head no, I was like, "You have to stay away from me there is a restraining order on you." But that didn't stop him from trying to talk me into pulling over. I was near my job, so I had to come to a stop. At that moment, He got out of the car and wanted to talk to me but I pulled out the restraining order and let him know this was real and I didn't want to be around him. He respected my wishes and left, but not without stating his case and trying to apologize.

I feel that because of where I was in my walk with the Lord and because of the armor I had put on that day it kept me from allowing the enemy to defeat me and cause me to cower down. I was no longer afraid but bold. I had to be firm and stern with him. I was able to look him in the eyes and let him know I meant business. This encounter is what led to the openness of forgiveness, so I could move forward with my life.

Now fast forward a little, me and the kids are living in peace, our life is finally back on track, and we are strong. We are in church faithfully and bringing some of the neighborhood kids along with us. I always had a heart for kids and if I could help them out in some way, I was going to do that. We are no longer living paycheck to paycheck; all our needs are met, and God is just loving on us and keeping us safe in His arms. God is also at work giving me good friends. My old crew wasn't my main crew anymore. He allowed me to associate and hang with them but not like I used to. But He gave me new friends that were on the same path as me. Friends who went to church with me and that would hold me accountable. I guess He was saying, "Okay Ashle', enough with just being with the kids, it's time to do more adult things." I won't lie I was comfortable with the kids and safe because I knew that they wouldn't betray me or abandon me as some people have done over the years.

But I am glad I obeyed and allowed Him to introduce me and even reintroduce me to people who I would be able to call friends and not associates. The people I found myself around were dependable, caring, loving, loyal, and inspiring. They didn't use me or talk about me but actually encouraged me and helped build me up. We had fun together and did things that would glorify God. We

Chapter 6: R&R (Rebuild & Restore)

read the Bible together and prayed for one another. The main difference between these friends versus the ones I had before was that God chose them, and I didn't. The season I was in called for kingdom friendships, not worldly ones. And that is no disrespect to my friends that are still in the world it was just that in order for me to be where I am now things had to shift. I still love those friends and pray for them all the time and I trust that in due time God will bring them home to Him so they can experience what I have been able to.

Now let's jump over to October 2017; a month that I will never forget, I won't bore you with all the specifics, but I had received a word from God a few months earlier while doing my evening or morning walk on the Singer Island Bridge. He whispered in my ear, "Move to Port St Lucie." A few days later He confirmed the word with a friend of mine. I was financially stable but not in a position to move just yet, I mean I just got a hold of how to manage my finances you know. This also meant moving away from my family and friends. So, long story short, I'm home working, my son is with his father getting a haircut, and my daughter just walked in from school all you hear next is... POP! POP! POP! POP! POP! I stop in the mid-track of work and say get on the ground now multiple times.

I go to my daughter and make sure she is okay and

once the shots are done; I look around the house to make sure everything is intact because those shots were too loud meaning they were close range. I wasn't sure what was going on but I alerted my kids' dad to what just happened and to use caution when bringing my son home. I hear the police arrive so I go outside to speak with them. They asked if my house was hit, and I tell them no. But come to find out it was, in my son's room right where he would be sitting playing his video game, two bullets came through the wall and hit the TV. God saved my son by interfering and having his dad get him from school to get a haircut.

Needless to say, that day we packed up and moved in with my mom. We never looked back except to pack up our belongings. The shooting wasn't targeted at us but at someone else in the neighborhood that lived close by. The shooter saw their target outside and started shooting at them. If my daughter had come into the house a minute later who knows if she would have been caught in the crossfire. We were rattled that night and I knew our time in Palm Beach County was coming to an end soon. God had already spoken, so it was time I obey.

Moving back in with my mom was a struggle because we had just become comfortable in our new environment. She had a two-bedroom apartment with only enough room for her and one extra person, so imagine how it felt that three people had to now share one room. But the kicker

Chapter 6: R&R (Rebuild & Restore)

was not only did we have to share the room, but I also had to work in the room. So, I spent most of my time cooped up in a room with limited space all day. Imagine how cramped the space was with work equipment, a bed, clothes, a TV, etc. We endured it though.

By June 2018, we moved into our home in Port St Lucie, FL. It was one of the best decisions ever made not only on a financial basis but also for my family. We moved into new territory to start a fresh life away from all the drama and baggage of the past. It was a safer environment for my son. We wouldn't have to look over our shoulders worrying about gunshots being fired. The neighborhood was quiet, and the people were kind. We were at peace.

I still worked the same job from home and a position opened up that I was interested in. I applied for the job years ago but was not selected. But when I applied this time, I got the job and the cool thing is that during the interview, the lady kept saying that it was something different about me. She remembered me from the last interview and was amazed to see such a transformation in my appearance and character. She told me the job was mine and was willing to extend my start date because I had some personal matters to attend to.

So, what took eight years to destroy was restored and repaired in a matter of four years. I graduated college with a BAS degree in Supervision and Management, and eventually started my own business. My daughter graduated high school and enlisted in the U.S. Navy. My son was able to enjoy his childhood in a better environment and improved significantly in school. Our story was and currently is being rewritten, but this time with God as the author. Now you can't tell me that God ain't good.

CHAPTER 7:
YOU ARE NOT ALONE

We often go through life with a me, myself, and I mentality. Feeling as if we are the only ones on the planet going through something. We think no one could ever understand the pain, the hurt, or the feelings that we have. And because of this, we choose to bottle up our feelings and just deal with life alone. We keep quiet and try to figure things out on our own and end up frustrated and hating life.

It's true that life may not start the way we would like, but that does not mean that it has to end that way. Family may treat you badly, you may be forced into uncomfortable situations, and things happen to us outside of our control. We make vows and promises to ourselves that we would never let these things get to us or become a part of our adult life and then.... boom life happens. We find ourselves being connected to the very thing we dislike and said we would never partake in.

I saw firsthand how the abuse had entered my family and even heard of stories before my time where people were abused by others. I was one of the ones who said once I grew up, I would never allow anyone else to mistreat me or even hit me. But the apple didn't fall too far from the tree, I fell into the same trap as those before me did. As I reflect on it, it's coming into perspective that this was a generational curse. Not only was I in an abusive cycle but I was being tormented spiritually and felt helpless. But with prayer and fasting, I have dealt with the root of this thing and pleaded the blood of Jesus over my bloodline so that abuse will be a thing of the past.

I did not feel safe or comfortable talking to many people because I just felt it wasn't their place and the news would be spread around. My mind was so conflicted because I wasn't thinking about my safety or the safety of my children. I was worried more about my reputation and causing harm to someone else. I never wanted to be the girl that sent someone to jail or brought harm to another human being. I just wanted peace and for everyone to get along. I wanted to follow the street code and handle my own situations myself. Even if that meant risking my own life.

Most often people who are victims of abuse feel as if they are alone and there is no way of escape. But I am here as proof that with faith and the right people on your side

Chapter 7: You Are Not Alone

that you can make it out. The news has been filled with so many domestic violence stories of women and even men being killed in relationships, children being abused by adults, and so much more. We watch these stories and feel like our situation is not that bad but, truth be told you could be next if you continue to stay in an unhealthy relationship.

I know that it is not easy to walk away from an abusive situation. So, I will never judge a person nor condemn a person that stays. But because of my history and experience, I would encourage you to pay attention to the signs and red flags. Don't allow yourself to be so wrapped up in a person that you began to lose yourself and life becomes all about them. You are important and you matter as well.

I spent years wondering why I allowed it and how could I have been so blind and dumb. I was afraid of what the world would say and didn't know how I could actually make it on my own without an abuser. I was lost and felt hopeless countless nights, just crying myself to sleep because I was weak and felt so vulnerable. I felt no good relationship would ever come to me because I was so used to people taking advantage of me and using me for their benefit. It was like people felt I was naïve and would just allow anything and for some time, I did. I made a lot of mistakes, even as a parent by putting my children in jeopardy all because of a lifestyle that was not truly satisfying. I felt like I had a lot to prove but in reality, I had a lot to lose.

I downplayed a lot of the abuse I experienced because I thought to myself it could be much worse. But ask yourself, is getting a black eye, busted lip, bite marks, scratches, cheated on, stolen from, and spoken down on make you feel good? Of course not, and no one deserves it no matter how messed up or bad you may view yourself. Abuse is abuse; no matter how we try to categorize it and it is WRONG. It should not be tolerated by anyone on any level.

Whoever told you that you have to stay and work it out was wrong. No one should stay where they are not safe and are at risk of dying all because of someone else insecurities. Yes, you may feel lonely, but you are not alone. You may even feel unworthy but you are valued. I remember many times looking into the mirror trying to understand the woman staring back at me. I didn't like what I saw because I was weak and I felt very ugly but I did have life in my body.

A mentor came to me one day and spoke some encouraging words to me. She told me that she sees me and that she experienced what I experienced. She told me that she loved me and wanted me to live. She said that I didn't need this baggage in my life and she could tell

Chapter 7: You Are Not Alone

I was tired. All I could do was just cry because she was speaking the truth. I wanted out, actually, I needed out because at this point, I felt like just dying to escape the embarrassment and pain.

I want to tell you the same thing that she told me. I love you and you are valued. I want to see you live because there are people who need you in this world. God did not create you so that you can be abused. God wants you to live an abundant life. He has so much in store for you, but in order to get what He has you have to make a decision. You are the apple of His eye and He sees you, the real you that no one else gets to experience.

You may be inconvenienced. I know I was when it came to having to leave my home and go to someone else home so that I could get a break. I would have to lie and make up excuses as to why I had to stay there. But I really just wanted to be at home in my own bed. I would have to sleep on people's couches and just feel so disgusted. I had a place I was paying rent for but couldn't stay there because it wasn't safe.

Find a close friend that you can confide in and that will be honest with you no matter what. Let them help you work on planning an exit strategy. Think about your children or family members that really do care for you. Develop a personal relationship with the Lord and ask Him to lead you in this dark season. Get plugged into a community of people who will encourage, strengthen, love, and care for you. Don't put the burden of doing life alone on yourself.

Seek the counsel of a therapist and a pastor. There are many solutions available and you never know what someone else is experiencing unless a conversation is had. Stop making excuses for why someone does what they do. I've done it many times. Be honest with yourself and tell the truth. And put yourself in someone else shoes and use the advice that you would give them. You know how we watch movies and have our own opinions and thoughts on what should be done? Look at your life through that same lens and do what you know you need to do… Walk away, please if not for yourself, I ask you to please do it for me.

PRAYER

As we come to the close of this book, I want to leave a prayer for those who are suffering silently:

Father God,

I come as a servant daughter of Yours, praying and interceding for my brother or sister who has read this book and found themselves in a cycle of abuse, as either an abuser or victim. I pray that today is a day of deliverance and freedom for them. You know the situation and the posture of their heart. I pray for them to have a divine encounter with You so that they can break free from this oppression of abuse. Just as I was trapped in the cycle of abuse, whether mental, physical, emotional, or financial, You set me free, and I know You can do the same for them. Help them to see themselves as You do, valuable and loved. Every word that has been spoken over them that is against Your will I bind it and rebuke it in Jesus's name. Every stronghold that tries to hold them back and keep them in this dark space I cancel and curse it at the root. Lord God, show them a way of escape and give them the courage, strength, and game plan on how to get out. Remove fear and replace it with faith. I pray they will yield to You and allow You full reign over their life. Send someone in their path that will bring light to their darkness and walk with them along this road to recovery. Show them that they are not alone and do not have to do this alone. Increase their boldness to take a stand and say no more to abuse. Father God, I ask that You help them to forgive their abusers or those who have wronged them. Help them to release the spirit of offense. Heal their brokenness and cover them with the blood of Jesus. For the abuser Lord, reveal to them their weaknesses and areas of bitterness, resentment, and hate. Teach them how to handle anger and not take it out on others. Send Your Holy Spirit to consume and take over each person and let them surrender all things to You. If they do not know You, I pray they will come to a place of repentance and seek forgiveness of their sins against You and others. I pray they will confess and accept that Jesus Christ is Lord over their life and that He died and rose again on the third day so that they may be saved. Lord, You are here to help all people, so I thank You in advance for changing the lives of my dear brothers and sisters. I seal this prayer with the power of the Holy Spirit and in the name of Jesus Christ.

Amen, Amen, and Amen!

AFTERWORD

Over the years, I have met so many people who have experienced some form of abuse and I would sit and talk with them and pray for them. It hurts me to my core when I see people suffering and feel like there is no hope. I begin to share my story with them so they get to see that there is life outside of abuse. And every time I share, they would just be blown away and say that I should write a book. They felt that people all over needed to hear and see what the Lord has done in my life. I apologize I couldn't give every single detail, but I pray that you took from this what the Lord needed you to.

It's so much that I went through a young age of thirty-seven, but I know that it was to help encourage and motivate others. I have learned the true value of love and I know that when the time comes for me to marry it will be destined by God. We can't be God in our lives we have to learn how to submit and allow His will to be done. It will be uncomfortable, just like writing this book was, but it is needed in order to complete the assignment we are called to. As I wrote this book my main focus was to help set people free and introduce them to the God I serve. And prayerfully that has been accomplished.

ABOUT THE AUTHOR

Ashle' Bell is a mother of two children, born and raised in the state of Florida, where she currently resides. She is a devout follower and believer in Jesus Christ. She loves serving and helping others when she is not spending time with her family and friends. She is in the finance industry and has a business as a Financial Fitness coach, helping others pursue financial freedom. You put some numbers in front of her and watch her get to work.

Ashle' loves some Jesus Music, that's a mixture of Gospel, Contemporary, and Christian Rap music. She serves as a youth ministry teacher and prayer intercessor at her local church. She loves a good book that will challenge, encourage, and teach her new things. She loves journaling her thoughts and prayers. She loves to travel and attend Kingdom events. To know her is to genuinely love her.